OSPREY COMBAT AIR

LANCASTER
SQUADRONS
1944-45

SERIES EDITOR: TONY HOLMES

OSPREY COMBAT AIRCRAFT • 35

LANCASTER SQUADRONS 1944-45

Jon Lake

OSPREY
PUBLISHING

Front Cover
Although Bomber Command's Lancaster squadrons would fly daylight attacks against German targets, as well as tactical missions against enemy positions and even pinpoint strikes on bridges, capital ships and other targets during the final 18 months of the war, night attacks against area targets in German cities remained their 'bread and butter'. Here, a Lancaster B III of No 576 Sqn (identifiable by the UL codes on its flanks) flies over a burning cityscape, a Pathfinder Lancaster approaching the target obliquely below, close to a cluster of burning green Target Indicators. The No 576 Sqn aircraft is, so far, high above the black flak bursts, its bomb-bay doors wide open and its crew tense, waiting for the bomb-aimer's terse 'Bombs Gone'.

Formed on 25 November 1943 from a nucleus provided by No 103 Sqn's C Flight, as well as a handful of crews from No 101 Sqn, No 576 Sqn was a No 1 Group Main Force bomber unit, based in Lincolnshire at Elsham Wolds and then at Fiskerton from October 1944. The squadron flew the first of its 189 wartime raids on 26/27 November 1943 – just 24 hours after its formation. The new unit sent its Lancasters against Berlin as part of a raid by 443 aircraft, 29 of which failed to return. The Battle of Berlin would cost the squadron nine Lancasters, but the unit continued to 'do its duty' by participating in many of Bomber Command's most significant attacks, losing one aircraft at Nuremberg and another during the infamous attack on Dresden. The squadron ended the war by participating in Operation *Manna*, dropping vital food supplies to the starving Dutch, and by ferrying home Allied troops and former PoWs after the end of hostilities.

No 576 Sqn lost 66 aircraft in the course of its 2788 wartime sorties, and six more were destroyed in flying accidents. Although many of its Lancasters enjoyed only short service lives, some three of the unit's aircraft survived more than 100 missions. No 576 Sqn disbanded on 19 September 1945 at Fiskerton (*cover artwork by Iain Wyllie*)

First published in Great Britain in 2002 by Osprey Publishing
Elms Court, Chapel Way, Botley, Oxford, OX2 9LP

© 2002 Osprey Publishing Limited

ISBN 1 84176 433 7

Edited by Tony Holmes
Page design by Tony Truscott
Cover Artwork by Iain Wyllie
Aircraft Profiles by Chris Davey
Origination by Grasmere Digital Imaging, Leeds, UK
Printed in China through Bookbuilders

02 03 04 05 06   10 9 8 7 6 5 4 3 2 1

EDITOR'S NOTE
To make this best-selling series as authoritative as possible, the Editor would be interested in hearing from any individual who may have relevant photographs, documentation or first-hand experiences relating to the world's combat aircraft, and the crews that flew them, in the various theatres of war. Any material used will be credited to its original source. Please write to Tony Holmes at 10 Prospect Road, Sevenoaks, Kent, TN13 3UA, Great Britain, or by e-mail at: tony.holmes@osprey-jets.freeserve.co.uk

ACKNOWLEDGEMENTS
The Editor wishes to thank Tony Iveson, Phil Jarrett, Frank Mason, Alastair McQuaid, Bruce Robertson and Nick Stroud at *Aeroplane* magazine for the provision of photographs for inclusion in this volume.

For a catalogue of all Osprey Publishing titles please contact us at:

Osprey Direct UK, PO Box 140, Wellingborough, Northants NN8 2FA, UK
E-mail: info@ospreydirect.co.uk

Osprey Direct USA, c/o MBI Publishing, 729 Prospect Ave, PO Box 1, Osceola, WI 54020, USA
E-mail: info@ospreydirectusa.com

Or visit our website: **www.ospreypublishing.com**

CONTENTS

INTRODUCTION

Together with the Spitfire and Hurricane, the Lancaster is one of the few RAF aircraft to be widely known by the general public, its exploits in World War 2 making the Avro bomber a truly legendary weapon of war which has entered the general history books.

The Lancaster dropped 608,612 tons of bombs during the war out of a Bomber Command wartime total of 955,044. This amounted to two-thirds of the RAF's total bomb tonnage dropped after January 1942. Lancasters flew 156,192 operational sorties during the war (nearly four times as many as the rival Halifax), including 107,085 on bombing raids against Germany. No fewer than 3836 Lancasters were lost, 2508 aircraft during operations against Germany itself. The Lancaster formed the backbone of Bomber Command's operational strength, equipping 56 frontline squadrons by war's end. Finally, Lancaster aircrew won ten of the thirty-two 'air' Victoria Crosses awarded during World War 2.

The Lancaster did carry a greater tonnage of bombs than any other bomber (as a whole, and per aircraft) as described in *Osprey Combat Aircraft 31 - Lancaster Units 1942-43*, and was able to carry a wider range of weapons, while it was also a joy to fly. The aircraft even retained its handling characteristics when heavily laden. In an air force run by pilots, being a great pilot's aircraft was of almost incalculable value, and pre-disposed the Air Staff to view the Lancaster in a more favourable light. But (again as described in the previous volume) the Avro bomber was a poor multi-role aeroplane, and a death trap for crews when hit by enemy fire.

The late-mark Halifax gave its crews a much better chance of survival, and proved more adaptable to other roles. But Air Chief Marshal Sir Arthur 'Bomber' Harris (AOC-in-C Bomber Command from early 1942 through to war's end) was always a scathing critic of the Halifax. He placed no value whatsoever on its multi-role versatility, and never bothered to re-evaluate the aircraft once he had formed his impression of the initial Merlin-engined version. Certainly, he gave no impression of realising that the aircraft suffered a lower loss rate than the Lancaster during early Pathfinder Force (PFF) operations (even in its Merlin engined form), nor that in its later radial-engined form during the latter part of the war, it enjoyed a considerably lower loss rate than the Lancaster (0.56 per cent compared to 0.74 per cent). The fact that 29 per cent of Halifax crews who were downed survived the experience, compared to only 11 per cent of Lancaster aircrew would have been of little interest to Harris, to whom live aircrew languishing in PoW camps were of little value.

What did matter to Harris was the tonnage of bombs dropped on the Reich (not necessarily accurately dropped on the target), and since the average Lancaster would drop 154 tons of bombs in its lifetime, while the average Halifax would drop only 100 tons, the Lancaster won the unshakeable confidence of Bomber Command's C-in-C.

It is no wonder then that Harris was inclined to describe the Lancaster as the greatest single factor in the Allied victory in World War 2. This was,

The man known to the press and public as 'Bomber' Harris was known to his intimates as 'Butch' or 'Bert', and even by his given name of Arthur. Harris was perhaps the greatest champion of the Lancaster, scorning all the other four-engined types available to him, and overseeing the creation of a force of 58 squadrons by VE-Day, with further units in the process of forming. Harris became an increasingly controversial figure, especially following the attacks on Dresden, although he won the loyalty and devotion of his aircrew *(Bruce Robertson)*

An anonymous crew from No 12 Sqn pose in front of 'their' Lancaster at Wickenby, in Lincolnshire, presumably for an end-of-tour photograph. If so, they were rather luckier than the crews of the 3349 Lancasters which failed to return from operations. The aircraft's individual code letter 'Q' is repeated on the nose, above the standard No 1 Group gas detection patch *(via Bruce Robertson)*

however, an extremely controversial view, although many historians and commentators have nevertheless accepted it without question.

In fact, the Lancaster's importance has been overstated, while even the impact of Bomber Command's overall campaign is highly questionable. The war of attrition against German industry and the German industrial workforce has often been misunderstood and has frequently been vociferously condemned, although it undeniably laid the foundations of the Allied victory. At the heart of this bloody war was the Avro Lancaster. By many measures, the Lancaster was the single most important aircraft type in Bomber Command, although the importance of the Pathfinder Mosquitos was arguably greater, although they were small in number and dropped fewer bombs. Some credit the Mosquito with ensuring the effectiveness of the more numerous Main Force 'heavies', and their much higher bomb tonnage.

The vital importance of the Mosquito bomber is described more fully in other volumes of this series, but it is perhaps interesting to note that the unarmed, high-speed 'Wooden Wonder' could be seen as representing the future, while the much lauded Lancaster was an aircraft which represented the end of an era – slow, with heavy defensive armament and a heavy bombload – a bludgeon in an era which was seeing the introduction of the rapier.

To have expected the Air Staff to have discarded its Trenchardian attachment to the doctrine of strategic bombing for morale effect when war broke out is probably unrealistic. It is, however, equally incomprehensible that even in the light of operational experience little attempt was made to shift the emphasis of the bombing campaign. The success of aircraft like the Whirlwind in cross-channel interdiction missions contrasted strongly with the lack of results achieved (and with the heavy losses incurred) by its heavy bomber contemporaries during the early years of the war, while even the hopeless Blenheim hit the enemy hard in cross-channel and shipping attacks, albeit at horrendous cost.

The contrast between the effectiveness of the Mosquito and Boston by comparison with the Lancaster, Halifax and Stirling was, if anything, even more marked. It was always the case that the smaller, faster, more survivable bombers were more likely to hit their targets than the four-engined 'heavies', and that their relatively tiny bombloads were thereby more effective. They were also much more likely to survive to attack targets again and again, while the large bombers were, for most of the war, statistically unlikely to complete even a single tour of operations.

The standard Heavy Bomber apologist's argument was that Heavy Bombers were the only way (or even the best way) of carrying the war to the enemy during the dark days of 1940-1943, but this argument does not bear close scrutiny. Everything achieved by the heavy bombers up to the end of 1943 could have been achieved equally well (or better) and at less cost by fighter-bombers and faster, more survivable light bombers.

Moreover, had Germany been forced to adequately defend tactical and strategic targets against the number of Whirlwinds, Bostons and Mosquitos that could have been procured for the cost of the Lancaster, the drain on resources and manpower would have been even greater. Some targets would have been out of range of even the Mosquitos (although these could reach Berlin with a worthwhile load), but the ability to hit any target in the Reich was never as vital as Harris pretended, and it must be acknowledged that Bomber Command's assault on the Reich capital was largely a costly failure.

Moreover, the relatively paltry investment made in aircraft like the Whirlwind before war broke out, and the massive resources devoted to mediocre and inferior heavy bombers was as much Harris's fault as

A snapshot of the senior personnel of an anonymous Lancaster station. Only 23 of the 41 men and women seen in the photograph wear the wings which set them apart as aircrew, including the air commodore in the centre and no fewer than three wing commanders – presumably the COs of the station's flying squadrons. Even by the end of the war, losses were such that one in three or four crews would fail to complete a tour of operations, and casualties among squadron commanders and other senior aircrew were even higher *(via Aeroplane)*

anyone else's, since he had been a member of the Air Staffs under which the RAF had attained its eve-of-war shape and structure.

There can thus be little doubt that the strategic air campaign against the Third Reich could have been fought better and more effectively, causing greater damage and costing fewer casualties, given the benefit of hindsight. But whether any commander of Harris' background and age could have realistically been expected to embrace the kind of innovative thinking that would have been required for a different bomber war to have been fought remains one of history's most fascinating 'might-have-beens'.

But while it may be unrealistic to have expected Harris to embrace the kind of bombing offensive outlined above, it is entirely reasonable to have expected him to have been rather more open-minded about the air war than he was. His opposition to any diversion of resources from 'his' private war against Germany was almost blindly wilful, and undeniably restricted and limited the success of Coastal Command's vital campaign to combat the U-boat menace, safeguard Allied convoys, and impose a blockade on Germany. It has been calculated that a single four-engined bomber allocated to Coastal Command (never viewed by Harris as anything better than a 'sideshow') had 20 times more effect on the German economy than the same aircraft allocated to Bomber Command. This is a contentious and controversial statistic, but it gives an idea of how important a part Coastal Command played in the defeat of Germany.

Similarly, Harris was never very willing to countenance the despatch of heavy bombers to overseas theatres, unless they were aircraft types which he felt were useless to Bomber Command, like the Liberator, which was thus 'spared' for use in the Middle East and India (and, of course, by Coastal Command). Fortunately for other Commands, Harris was as blind to the attributes of some aircraft as he was to the importance of other ways of winning the war. Thus the Liberator was discarded by Bomber Command because of its modest payload and altitude, while its phenomenal range and good defensive armament were ignored.

The first Lancaster volume in this series covered the aircraft's conception, genesis and introduction, and its combat record during 1942-43. This early period marked a transition from costly (and largely futile) raids by relatively small numbers of aircraft to mass raids which actually hit the Germans hard, although the loss rate would remain alarmingly high, and bombing accuracy poor throughout 1943. Even the individual high-profile episodes, like the Augsburg and Dams raids described in the first volume, were largely costly but heroic 'failures'.

Early Lancaster operations had often been hopelessly inaccurate, frequently inflicting a handful of civilian casualties and destroying a couple of houses at the cost of several aircraft and their precious crews. But while attacks on area targets

An unidentified airman in the cockpit of an equally anonymous Lancaster (although the 'sainted' bomb log may give some clue to the veteran bomber's identity), photographed by the legendary Charles E Brown. The 'erks' laboured long and hard in often appalling conditions to keep their aircraft in top condition, and if some occasionally succumbed to the temptation of having a photo taken in the cockpit of 'their' aircraft, who could blame them? *(via Phil Jarrett)*

continued to form the Lancaster's 'bread and butter', accuracy improved exponentially, until what Bomber Command regarded as area attacks were often more accurate (saturating the aim point) than what the USAAF thought were pinpoint 'precision attacks'. This was especially true when poor weather intervened to prevent pure visual bomb-aiming, and when the USAAF's bombardiers had to forsake their much-vaunted Norden bombsights for H_2S bombing radar, in whose use they were much less well trained than their RAF counterparts.

Germany's Armaments Minister, Albert Speer, commented that 'The RAF night attacks are considerably more effective than the US daylight attacks, since heavier bombs are used, and extraordinary accuracy in attacking the target is reported'.

Moreover, the Lancaster and its crews also performed some of the most daring and exciting pinpoint attack missions of the war, and the 'exchange rate' of crews lost to damage inflicted was transformed so that bomber and bomber crew losses were finally more than balanced by the horrific destruction and carnage which they wreaked.

However, it would be mistaken to view the Bomber Command campaign as anything other than a meat-grinder for RAF aircrew, even during the last 18 months of the war, and although their effectiveness dramatically increased, they continued to suffer heavy (if reducing) losses, and from time to time were forced to abandon attacks against particular targets.

Even in 1942-43, the Lancaster had enjoyed a clear advantage over the RAF's other frontline bomber types. Aircraft like the Stirling and Halifax had been designed during peacetime, whereas the Lancaster was designed in wartime, drawing on the light of real operational experience. Peacetime requirements for multi-role capability and a 100-ft wingspan (to fit inside the RAF's standard hangar) could be ignored, and greater emphasis could be placed on the type's ease and economy of production. The aircraft was

Twenty Lancaster centre sections can be seen in this view of the Armstrong Whitworth production line at Baginton, in Warwickshire, in 1944 – just one of the plants which churned out Lancasters to meet Bomber Command's voracious appetite for new aircraft. A total of 7377 Lancasters were built, and nearly half of these were lost on operations, with many more being written off in accidents *(via Phil Jarrett)*

Radial-engined B IIs accounted for only a tiny percentage of Lancaster production, with 301 aircraft built. Of these, only 51 survived the rigours of operations (in which 179 were lost) and accidents (which claimed another 71). Only ten aircraft remained serviceable (of 16 on charge with the Heavy Conversion Units) by the time the war ended, and the type was declared obsolete *(via Aeroplane)*

optimised for bomber operations, and as a bomber it was clearly superior to the Stirling or early Merlin-engined versions of the Halifax.

Things would get very much better for Bomber Command during 1944 and into 1945, largely thanks to the widespread adoption of improvements and new technology, much of which had actually been introduced on a smaller scale during the early years. The Lancaster itself had already dominated Bomber Command by the end of 1943, out-numbering all other four-engined bombers put together, and this dominance and importance was only reinforced during 1944-45.

But by late 1944 the Lancaster's advantages were less clear-cut. By comparison with the radial-engined Halifax III (and especially the later B VI and B VII) the Lancaster suffered a higher loss rate, and its crews were more likely to die if their aircraft was shot down. The Lancaster could still drop its bombs from higher altitude, and could still carry a heavier bombload further into the Reich, but some believe that the Lancaster crews, bombing from higher altitude, in greater discomfort, further from base, over more heavily defended 'heartland' targets like Berlin, may have been rather less accurate in delivering their bombs.

But in Arthur Harris's strategic bombing campaign large numbers of inaccurate bombs dropped on 'area targets' in the vicinity of Berlin were worth more than smaller tonnages of bombs which were dropped more accurately on pinpoint targets closer to home. Live Halifax aircrew who bailed out 'into the cage' (enemy PoW camps) were no more useful to Harris than dead Lancaster aircrew, so mere survival rates meant little, while the Halifaxes' multi-role capabilities were viewed as being at best irrelevant, and at worst a potential reason for bombers to be diverted into what Harris regarded as 'secondary' roles and theatres.

It was this hostility to 'diversion' that led to the Lancaster's extraordinary success in the tactical role being widely overlooked. In the run-up to and immediate aftermath of Operation *Overlord*, Bomber Command switched much of its attention to hitting tactical targets in France, and proved extremely effective, though HQ Bomber Command committed its aircraft to such operations with reluctance, and itched to return its 'Heavies' to what it saw as the 'serious business of winning the war'.

Moreover, few senior officers at Group Headquarters, or at Bomber Command HQ at High Wycombe had first hand experience of the new Halifax versions, and the Handley Page aircraft was judged on the record of the inferior Merlin-engined variants which many of them had flown, and which had never been a match for the Lancaster.

But the poor performance of the early Merlin-powered Halifax had sealed its fate, and Bomber Command increasingly moved towards becoming an all-Lancaster force, at least insofar as frontline bomber squadrons were concerned. The Lancaster's widespread use amounted to virtual dominance by the war's end. By 1945, Bomber Command included 56 frontline Lancaster squadrons, and could routinely call upon around 750 frontline aircraft. Production was sufficient to allow Bomber Command to replace losses, re-equip training units and even to begin to re-equip Halifax and Stirling units. Even the second-string Bomber Groups in Yorkshire were beginning to re-equip with Lancasters as the war drew to a close. Only the spectre of operations in the Far East promised any future for the Halifax, which was better suited to tropical operations.

Once the War was over, concentrating on a single bomber type was even more important, and the Halifax and Stirling quickly faded from the scene, leaving the Lancaster and Lincoln briefly dominant before the advent of the first jet bombers.

The Lancaster and Lincoln (and the Lancaster's transport derivative, the York) flew on for some years after the war, and played an active part in several more wars and combat operations, but that, as they say, is another story.

The Lancaster was an undeniably important and effective weapon of war, albeit one which could have been used more effectively. It is hard to argue that many of Bomber Command's 55,000 dead were not

The 7377th Lancaster? This aircraft (TX273) was certainly the last Lancaster to be completed at Avro's Yeadon plant (in October 1945), and had the 'highest' serial number allocated to any Lancaster, but it may not have been the last to fly, since the final example built by Armstrong Whitworth (TW911) was delivered to the RAF some five months later *(via Aeroplane)*

squandered in a strategic bombing campaign that was wasteful and largely ineffective. Had the four engined heavies been used in larger numbers in the war against the U-boat menace, and in tactical operations like those which led up to and accompanied D-Day, leaving the strategic campaign until the Luftwaffe had been defeated, losses would have been much lighter. Had the industrial capacity and manpower expended on the 'wasted' aircraft been used instead on aircraft like the Westland Whirlwind and de Havilland Mosquito, the damage to German industrial and military targets would have been greater and losses would have been lighter.

But the way in which Harris used the Lancaster was crude, profligate and extravagant. Small wonder that the Luftwaffe's chief of staff, General Jeschonnek, was moved to remark that 'Every four-engined bomber the Western Allies build makes me happy, for we will bring these down just as we brought down the two-engined ones, and the destruction of a four-engined bomber constitutes a much greater loss to the enemy'. It is hard to imagine that Jeschonnek would have been so calmly accepting had the RAF been launching nightly raids by thousands of Mosquitos and Whirlwind fighter-bombers.

But the strategy followed by the Air Staff favoured the despatch of much larger, heavier bombers in huge numbers, bombing with relatively little precision from great height, and usually by night. It may have been the wrong strategy, but there can be no doubt that having embarked on a night area bombing offensive, the Lancaster was the right aircraft to carry it out.

A great pilot's aircraft, the Lancaster suffered a lower loss rate than any of its contemporaries (with the exception of the Mosquito and the very last Halifax variants) and by the end of the war was able to wreak huge destruction on the enemy. Had the war lasted longer in the Far East, the Lancaster might have had further opportunities to show its mettle, but as things were, the early post-war conflicts involving the RAF tended to involve its successor, the Lincoln, and the Lancaster enjoyed a relatively peaceful run-down until its final retirement.

But post-war use of the Lancaster, and of the improved Lincoln (once known as the Lancaster B IV) and the transport York will be more properly tackled in a separate volume in the Combat Aircraft series.

Target – Germany! Trundling along the perimeter track on only two engines in order to save fuel, Lancasters taxi out to the runway in the gathering gloom as 'erks' make their way back from their dispersals on their trusty bicycles. This was a sight repeated thousands of times at Bomber Command's eastern aerodromes. Hours later the survivors would return, only to repeat the process the following evening *(via Phil Jarrett)*

THE BATTLE OF BERLIN

The Battle of Berlin began in earnest on the night of 18/19 November 1943, and Bomber Command had mounted an additional eight raids against the German capital by month-end (on 18/19, 22/23, 23/24 and 26/27 November). Four more raids followed in December (2/3, 16/17, 23/24 and 29/30 December). The battle then continued into 1944, thus straddling the time periods covered in the two volumes of this Osprey history of the RAF's wartime Lancaster force.

Although the Battle of Berlin began during late 1943, it reached its zenith in early 1944, and is thus described in this volume, rather than being divided between this volume and the previous one.

Despite the heavy losses suffered and negligible results achieved during 1942-43, Arthur Harris had been disproportionately buoyed by the success of the Hamburg raids and the effectiveness of the pinpoint attack on Peenemünde. He continued to believe that Germany could be defeated through bombing alone, and set his sights on reducing the German capital to rubble.

'We can wreck Berlin from end to end if the USAAF will come in on it. It will cost us between 400-500 aircraft. It will cost Germany the War', Harris told Churchill, and in a letter to the Air Ministry on 7 December 1943 claimed that he could destroy Berlin, and bring the war to an end, by 1 April 1944. Harris described the aim of his attacks on Berlin as

This No 12 Sqn Lancaster B III (LM321) was a much travelled machine, passing from unit to unit. It flew against Berlin on 3/4 September 1943 with No 12 Sqn, and then again on 26/27 November and 2/3 December with No 460 Sqn, and on 29/30 December with No 550 Sqn. The aircraft was lost on the 10/11 June 1944 raid on Acheres, by when it had passed to No 100 Sqn *(via Phil Jarrett)*

being 'to cause the heart of the German nation to stop beating', and felt disinclined to apologise for directly targeting the enemy civilian population. When pressed to use a higher proportion of incendiaries, he argued the case for high explosive (HE), saying, 'I do not agree with this policy. The morale effect of HE is vast. People can escape from fires, and the casualties on a solely fire raising raid would be as nothing.

What we want to do in addition to the horrors of fire is to bring the masonry crashing down on top of the Boche, to kill the Boche and to terrify the Boche'.

Berlin was an undeniably attractive target for Harris. Of enormous symbolic value as the capital of the Reich, Berlin also housed the inner workings of the Nazi machinery of government and all of the vital ministries that ran the German war machine. Berlin was also a hugely important industrial centre, with a number of tank, aircraft engine, instrument and machine tool factories and one quarter of Germany's electrical engineering industry. The city was also a vitally important communications hub between the Western and Eastern Fronts, and was the third largest city in the world, making it an ideal morale target.

Had Bomber Command been able to wreak the same level of destruction upon Berlin as it had done on Hamburg, some historians believed that Harris could have brought the war to premature end. But Berlin was not Hamburg, and it was never likely that Bomber Command would be able to hit it anything like so hard, or to such devastating effect.

While Hamburg was a coastal city and port (and thus the perfect H_2S target) lying just over 450 miles from Lincoln, Berlin was 150 miles further inside Germany, and well inland. It thus demanded an overland approach which would necessitate flying through miles of hostile and heavily defended airspace, well beyond the range of *Oboe*. Berlin was also a poor target for H_2S, stretching Bomber Command's navigational capabilities to the limit, even after the introduction of G-H in November 1943.

The RAF's inability to use *Oboe* for target marking has subsequently been blamed for the failure of the assault on Berlin by many expert analysts. The city was also far enough from Bomber Command's East Anglian bases to force some uneasy compromises for the Lancaster squadrons, with a need to balance bombload, performance, range and armour. It was also a massive, sprawling city, whose

Lancasters were kept in the open, dispersed around Bomber Command's frequently wind-scoured airfields. Conditions for the groundcrew were harsh and primitive, and protective clothing was a useful if uncommon luxury. The process of re-arming and refuelling aircraft was labour intensive, as seen in this image of groundcrew manoeuvring a bomb trolley at No 467 Sqn's Waddington home *(via Phil Jarrett)*

Incendiaries, high explosive 1000-lb bombs and a 4000-lb 'Cookie' wait to be loaded aboard a No 75 (NZ) Sqn Lancaster. The aircraft's unusual code presentation, with JN ahead of the roundel, is noteworthy *(via Phil Jarrett)*

important targets could easily be missed without accurate marking, and, as the Reich capital, it was very heavily defended.

Moreover, Hamburg had been attacked in summer weather, before missions began to be affected by cloud cover over the target, and before the German nightfighter arm had really developed adequate counters to the latest advances in Bomber Command's technology and equipment.

By the time Bomber Command embarked on its campaign against Berlin, taking advantage of longer winter nights, the weather was often poor and defences had improved. The new SN-2 *Lichtenstein* radar was in widespread service, and German nightfighter crews and their controllers had developed and refined new *Zähme Sau* (Tame Boar) tactics, using radar-equipped nightfighters in a more flexible and autonomous fashion, being vectored to the bomber stream where they then found and engaged their own targets.

This marked a move away from the rigid system of 'boxes' which a bomber stream could quite easily overwhelm, or could disrupt through jamming or the judicious use of 'Window', echoing the way in which single-engined day fighters had roamed freely under the *Wilde Sau* tactics developed to compensate for their lack of radar.

By February 1944, the Luftwaffe had deployed 200 SN-2 radar sets (which were better able to differentiate between real targets and 'Window'), and most of these were available for the later stages of the Battle of Berlin. The Germans also introduced new means of trying to 'turn night into day', making even greater use of searchlights and using high flying Ju 88s to drop parachute flares above the bomber stream.

Worse still, the Luftwaffe had discovered Bomber Command's primitive *Monica* tail warning radar, and H$_2$S had also been similarly compromised when shot down aircraft fell into German hands. It was a relatively easy matter to develop and deploy the *Flensburg* homer (which allowed a nightfighter pilot to home onto a *Monica*-equipped bomber) and the *Naxos-Z*, which could detect and locate H$_2$S emissions.

Only 28 enemy fighters were equipped with *Naxos-Z*, but there were also ground-based systems which could detect and roughly locate H$_2$S, while the way in which it was used (or more accurately over-used) also imposed some vulnerabilities. This was because decoy raids often used aircraft without H$_2$S, while the real raiders used H$_2$S intensively for route navigation and for target finding. This sometimes allowed German controllers to

L7532 was only the sixth production Lancaster ever built, and it subsequently saw service with Nos 44 (to whom it was delivered new on 28 December 1941), 97, 61, 50, 207 and 90 Sqns, before joining No 3 Lancaster Finishing School and eventually No 1656 Conversion Unit, as seen here. Truly a combat veteran, this aircraft was finally struck off charge on 16 October 1946 *(via Phil Jarrett)*

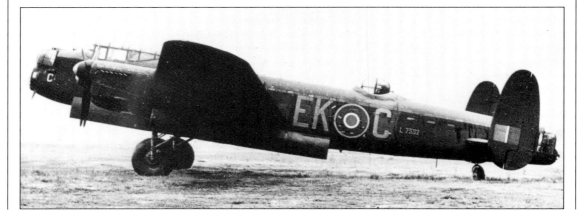

Hundreds of incendiaries topple from the bomb-bay of an ABC-equipped (note the two poles atop the fuselage) Lancaster of No 101 Sqn. These 'jamming specialists' routinely flew with a full bombload while protecting the Main Force bombers by disrupting enemy fighter control radio frequencies *(via Bruce Robertson)*

ignore spoof raids and concentrate their efforts on the vulnerable Main Force bombers. These new devices effectively turned *Monica* and H_2S into homing beacons for enemy fighters, while there was also equipment which could detect a bomber's IFF (identification friend or foe) transmissions.

As if this was not bad enough, an increasing number of nightfighters were equipped with upward firing 20 mm or 30 mm cannon (known as *Schräge Musik* – literally sloping music – or jazz). These allowed a nightfighter to sit underneath a bomber (in its blindspot) and pour a concentrated stream of fire into its unprotected belly, bomb-bay and fuel tanks. Only the handful of bombers equipped with FN 64 ventral turrets or improvised belly machine guns had any counter to this devastating weapon. Sometimes, a *Schräge Musik* equipped nightfighter could approach a bomber unseen, swimming up from below the aircraft unnoticed by the tail gunner.

But the bomber war was always a shifting pattern of measure and countermeasure, and the Battle of Berlin saw the RAF make its first use of a number of new devices that were intended to disrupt German nightfighter operations, although it was not until some way into the battle, on 23 November 1943, that the RAF's dedicated Bomber Support organisation, No 100 Group, was officially formed.

At the time of the Battle of Berlin, arguably the most important of these countermeasures was *Airborne Cigar* (ABC), since the later *Airborne Grocer* and *Jostle* systems were still in development. This was carried by some of No 101 Sqn's Main Force Lancasters, and consisted of a high-powered VHF jammer, targeted against the 38-42 megacycle FuG 16ZY radio used by the Germans for transmitting a 'running commentary' of the Bomber Stream's position, course and altitude. ABC was also used for jamming the *Benito* navigation aid used by enemy nightfighters. ABC would eventually be fitted to No 100 Group Fortresses and Halifaxes, but not in time for the Battle of Berlin. Fortunately, No 101 Sqn, a regular No 1 Group unit, began ABC operations in October 1943.

No 101 Sqn's ABC Lancasters were usually flown with a full bombload, and were visually identifiable from the array of twin vertical masts mounted on the aircraft's spine, and by a third antenna below the nose. Internally, the aircraft carried three separate jammers, with a Special Operator carried as an eighth crewmember. This German linguist found enemy transmissions, listened to them to ascertain whether they were fighter control frequencies and then tuned his jammers into them, suppressing the signal to see whether new frequencies were being used, and if necessary, jamming those too. But this was far too little to cope with the requirement for communications jamming, and could make only a local difference in parts of the bomber stream, jamming some of the enemy frequencies.

Because No 101 Sqn's ABC-equipped Lancasters accompanied every Main Force raid, the squadron expanded to meet its heavy commitments, with 36 and later 42 aircraft – plus four reserves. Bombers also used *Mandrel* to jam German *Freya* early warning radar, and 'Tinsel' to broadcast engine noise over fighter control frequencies. The squadron frequently despatched 30 aircraft in a single night, and (because their transmissions could be detected by enemy fighters) suffered heavy casualties – it lost 21 aircraft and 168 aircrew during the first ten weeks of the Battle of Berlin.

The bombers could also count on some limited fighter support, at least until the end of 1943, with *Serrate*-equipped Mosquitos and Beaufighters using their equipment to home onto the air intercept radar carried by enemy nightfighters, and with other Mosquitos flying 'Flower' missions (attacks against enemy nightfighter airfields as the enemy aircraft took off, while the Bomber Stream crossed the coast). Other radar-equipped Mosquitos flew *Mahmoud* patrols, flying straight and level to simulate a stray bomber then using *Monica* to detect an approaching enemy nightfighter before turning to get onto the enemy aircraft's tail.

The fighters enjoyed a number of successes, but there were too few to do more than complicate the lives of the enemy nightfighter crews, demoralising some of them, and perhaps causing a higher accident rate as enemy aircrew flew at lower level while preparing to land. But the *Nachtjagdwaffe* was at the peak of its powers, with the best equipment it had ever had, and not yet being attrited by being thrown into suicidal daylight operations against the 'Mighty Eighth'. The RAF nightfighters were unable to materially affect the enemy nightfighters' sortie rate, nor to make a real difference to the dangers facing the bomber aircrews.

Another enemy faced by the Lancaster crews was the winter weather, which made life more uncomfortable, and made navigation more difficult. Even if a bomber fought its way to and from the target unscathed, avoiding enemy night intruders that sometimes waited near the bomber aerodromes, the weather could be deadly. The low lying bomber airfields in East Anglia, Lincolnshire and Yorkshire were often affected by fog, and aircraft (especially damaged ones) often came to grief in these conditions. Fortunately, the winter of 1943 saw the introduction of a new system known as FIDO (Fog Investigation and Dispersal Operation) at 15 (mainly Bomber Command) bases – Blackbushe in Hampshire, Bradwell Bay in Essex, Carnaby in Yorkshire, Downham Market in Norfolk, Fiskerton in Lincolnshire, Foulsham in Norfolk, Gravely in Huntingdonshire, Ludford Magna in Lincolnshire, Manston in Kent, Melbourne in Yorkshire, Metheringham in Lincolnshire, St Eval in Cornwall, Sturgate in Lincolnshire, Tuddenham in Suffolk and Woodbridge in Suffolk.

The three main Emergency Landing Grounds – Carnaby in Yorkshire, Sutton Heath (Woodbridge) in Suffolk and Manston in Kent – were fitted with enlarged versions of FIDO because of the size of their runways.

The FIDO system fed fuel under pressure along pipes beside the main runway, where it was vaporised, and the vapour was then burned to thermally disperse convection fog, creating a clear 'tunnel' in which aircraft could land.

Bombers would still divert to airfields which were clear of fog where possible, but FIDO allowed aircraft to land safely where this could not be achieved. Woodbridge alone saw about 1200 safe landings using FIDO –

Armourers load a 4000-lb 'Cookie' into the cavernous bomb-bay of an unidentified Lancaster. The contemporary Keystone Press Agency caption released with this photograph on 20 November 1943 proudly announced that 'This Block Buster Fell On Berlin', describing it as 'four thousand pounds of high explosive freight . . . for delivery to Berlin'. The ability of the Lancaster to swallow even the largest bomb loads was the main feature which appealed to Bomber Command's chief *(via Aeroplane)*

The Hercules-engined B II was heavily used during the Battle of Berlin. Here, No 514 Sqn C Flt aircraft LL728 draws some interest after 'landing away' at a Wellington base. Its FN 64 ventral gun turret and bulged bomb-bay doors are clearly visible. A veteran of two raids on Berlin, LL728 was lost on the 26/27 August 1944 mission to Kiel *(via Phil Jarrett)*

of a wartime total of 2486 safe landings using the system.

Using a runway equipped with FIDO was by no means straightforward, however, because convection from the heat of the fires could make the landing approach very bumpy and turbulent, while enemy Ju 88 night intruders sometimes attacked aircraft that had been silhouetted by the flares lining the runway. FIDO was also extremely costly, burning 250,000 gallons of fuel at a cost of £42,500 every hour. FIDO remained in use at Manston (as a standby for London airport) until 1949, after which radar and ILS (Instrument Landing System) equipment had improved so much that the primitive FIDO system could be entirely phased out.

But FIDO could only minimise a proportion of Bomber Command's casualties, and all the ingredients were in place for a bloodbath when Harris finally launched his assault on Berlin, although things could easily have been worse. In terms of cost and effectiveness, the offensive against Berlin was destined to show how little things had changed, yet in other respects, Berlin deserves to be seen as marking the beginning of a new phase in Bomber Command's offensive.

Several older Bomber Command stalwarts were withdrawn immediately before or during the Battle of Berlin, including the Wellington, which flew its last raid on 8/9 October 1943. Ironically, the Wellington was ironically capable of toting a 4000-lb 'Cookie' all the way to Berlin – something that the Stirling could not do.

An ever increasing proportion of the Bomber Force was equipped with the Lancaster, including a number of new units flying radial-engined B IIs. Joining Nos 115 and 426 Sqns were two RCAF units, Nos 408 and 432 Sqns, which converted in August and September, and No 514 Sqn RAF.

The radial-engined interim B II had been developed in case of a disruption in the supply of the Lancaster's favoured Merlin engine, as the supply of US-supplied Packard Merlins could not then be absolutely guaranteed. The aircraft's relatively poor ceiling led to unfavourable comparisons being made by aircrew used to the Lancaster B I, but it was a superb replacement for Wellingtons or Stirlings. Moreover, the aircraft's air-cooled radial engines were much less vulnerable to battle damage, and, as a further bonus, the type enjoyed much better ditching characteristics.

Crucially, at least insofar as its crews were concerned, the Lancaster B II was also superior to the Merlin-engined version in almost

every area of performance except ceiling, as No 432 Sqn's Flg Off Jim McIntosh remembers;

'These things went like skinned cats! I bet we could out-run the bloody fighters. We had to concede to the Is and IIIs a bit on the bombing altitude, but on anything else we were better. Faster, quicker off the deck, less exhaust glow at night, no glycol and less engine trouble.'

Although the B II had a smaller bombload than the B I, most were fitted with bulged bomb doors which allowed it to carry an 8000-lb weapon. Moreover, early suggestions that the aircraft might be used for day bombing had led to provision for an FN 64 ventral gun turret, manned by an eighth crew member. Some squadron commanders retained the turret while others had it removed. Whether or not the turret was actually carried, the B II could not carry H_2S bombing radar, and so was used to pioneer the use of G-H.

This proved extremely effective during early operations, including an attack against the Mannesmann steel works near Düsseldorf on

An 8000-lb bomb is towed behind a ubiquitous David Brown tractor to a waiting Lancaster, which will in turn take the weapon on a one-way trip to Berlin. Harris favoured the use of high explosives over incendiaries, both for their lethality and their psychological effect
(via Phil Jarrett)

This No 426 Sqn B II (DS689/OW-S, illustrated in profile form in the previous Lancaster Combat Aircraft volume) flew against Berlin, but was lost during a raid on Stuttgart on 7/8 December 1943
(via Phil Jarrett)

3/4 November 1943. The equipment lacked the range to be useful against Berlin, however, and was removed from Main Force aircraft pending a return to shorter range operations.

The Lancaster IIs were heavily used during the Battle of Berlin, but with production of the type ending in March 1944, there were insufficient aircraft to replace losses, and the type began to disappear from the frontline. No 432 Sqn converted to the Halifax III in February 1944 and No 115 followed between March and May.

Although known as the Battle of Berlin, the period covering the winter of 1943-44 saw Bomber Command attacking a number of different targets. Had Harris attempted to attack Berlin every night (or even only when the weather permitted such attacks) losses would have reduced Bomber Command to no more than a cadre within days. Moreover, by dividing his attacks between Berlin and other targets Harris made it impossible for the Luftwaffe to concentrate its nightfighters in defence of Berlin, giving his bombers some element of surprise. Thus attacks on Berlin were interspersed with raids on other major targets, and were accompanied by feints and diversionary attacks, some of which used 'Window' to appear much larger than they really were. Some diversionary raids were flown by Mosquitos, although these appeared so fast to German radar operators that they were often accepted for what they were, and were simply ignored.

Dating the Battle of Berlin presents the historian with some problems, since the main offensive was preceded by a number of 'dress rehearsals'. The first of these took place on the night of 23/24 August 1943, led by Wg Cdr Johnny Fauquier, CO of No 405 Sqn, who acted as Master Bomber – 17 of the 335 Lancasters sortied were lost, together with 23 Halifaxes and 16 Stirlings. Overall, 56 aircraft, or 7.9 per cent of the 727 despatched, failed to return. The Pathfinders found it hard to find Berlin using H_2S and marked an area in the southern suburbs, resulting in the Main Force attacking southern residential areas and 25 nearby villages more than the city centre, although every building in the Wilhelmstrasse received some damage. Casualties totalled 684 civilians killed, plus 66 service and air raid personnel, 102 foreign workers and two PoWs. Large numbers of the dead had ignored instructions to use their air raid shelters, and paid the price for this.

After attacks on Nuremberg and Monchengladbach/Rheydt on 27/28 and 30/31 August, another rehearsal was flown on 31 August/ 1 September. This involved 331 Lancasters out of a total force of 622 bombers. Ten Lancasters were lost, along with 20 Halifaxes and 17 Stirlings, while the Pathfinders' marking was again well south of the target area, resulting in overall damage being limited to 85 houses destroyed and seven industrial build-ings damaged. Some 66 civilians

Another No 426 Sqn Lancaster II coded OW-S, DS830 had flown at least five missions against Berlin with No 432 Sqn prior to being passed to its second Canadian owner. The aircraft sortied to Berlin twice more (on 15/16 February and 24/25 March) with its new unit prior to being transferred to yet another Canadian unit, No 408 Sqn. Here it remained until mid-1944, when DS830 was relegated to training duties with No 1668 CU – the bomber was finally struck off charge on 20 March 1945. In this photograph, Flt Lt F R Shedd and Sgt T F Jones chat with groundcrew soon after completing a raid on Frankfurt on 22 March 1944. 33 bombers were lost on this particular night out of a force of 816 *(via Bruce Robertson)*

and two soldiers were killed, 109 were injured and 2784 were bombed out, prompting Gauleiter Goebbels to order the evacuation of all children and all those not engaged in war work. The effectiveness of the German defences came as an unpleasant surprise, as did the use of air dropped flares to illuminate the bombers.

A final 'practice' was undertaken on 3/4 September by 316 Lancasters and four Mosquitos, with the Stirlings and Halifaxes left behind after their heavy losses in the earlier raids. Even so, 22 Lancasters were lost (seven per cent of the force), although industrial targets were harder hit, with the bombing knocking out one of Berlin's biggest breweries, an electricity station and a major water works. The 422 dead included 225 civilians and 123 foreign workers.

Another precursor to the Battle of Berlin 'proper' was the mission flown against the Mannesmann steel works near Düsseldorf on 3/4 November. During this mission, Flt Lt Bill Reid of No 61 Sqn, flying a Merlin-engined Lancaster B III (LM360), won the VC.

Reid's Lancaster was attacked by a Bf 110, which was eventually driven off by the rear gunner, whose hands had become so cold that he was initially unable to give warning of the fighter's approach, nor to return fire. The Messerschmitt was thus able to inflict heavy damage on the Lancaster, knocking out the rear turret, the intercom, the compass and the trim tabs, and wounding Reid in the head, shoulders and hands. He nevertheless pressed on with his assigned mission, saying nothing of his injuries to the rest of the crew.

The bomber was then attacked by an Fw 190 which knocked out the oxygen system, hit the mid-upper turret and killed the navigator, as well as wounding the flight engineer and the wireless operator, the latter fatally. Reid continued on to the target, supplied with emergency oxygen by his wounded flight engineer, dropped his bombs accurately on the aim point, then set course for home, steering by the Pole star and the moon.

The pilot then lapsed into semi-consciousness and the flight engineer and bomb aimer flew the aircraft back across the North Sea, Reid reviving enough to land safely at the USAAF base at Shipdham, in Norfolk, despite mist and being partially blinded by blood from his head wound. The aircraft's undercarriage collapsed due to damage received during the attacks, but the crew avoided further injury. Both Reid and his Lancaster returned to operations, LM360 being written off in a crash landing at Fiskerton in November 1944.

The assault on Berlin 'proper' began on 18/19 November 1943, when Bomber Command despatched 416 Lancasters against the Reich capital, with 33 more, plus 362 Stirlings and Halifaxes, attacking Mannheim. The Mannheim force included 17 aircraft from No 7 Sqn, operating as Pathfinders, and seven B IIs from No 514 Sqn jamming with *Mandrel* and improved 'Tinsel'. The secondary raid did have the desired effect of confusing the enemy defences, and the loss of nine of the aircraft attacking Berlin was regarded as being remarkably light. Two more were lost on the Mannheim raid. The newly converted No 432 Sqn did not participate in the raid itself, but four aircraft did fly over the North Sea keeping watch for ditched aircraft and crews, and listening for distress calls.

Target marking was poor, however, and bombing was widely scattered as a result, and damage to the city was relatively slight. Too many

Pathfinder navigators had relied on spotting the River Spree with H_2S, and when they could not, dropped their markers by dead reckoning.

The second attack against Berlin was launched on 22/23 November, and this time the PFF marked the target impeccably, and significant damage was inflicted on an industrial plant as well as a number of city landmarks, including the Kaiser Wilhelm Gedächtniskirche, the Berlin Zoo, the Charlottenburg Castle and the Unter den Linden. No fewer than 3000 houses were totally destroyed and 175,000 people were bombed out, with casualties topping 2000 people, including 500 in one single massive shelter and 105 in another. 50,000 troops (equivalent to three full Divisions) were sent to the city to help with the clean-up operation. Eleven Lancasters (of 469 despatched) failed to return, although there was no secondary or diversionary raid. Five Stirlings were lost on the raid (of 50 sent out), and the type was immediately withdrawn from further Main Force operations to German targets.

When Bomber Command launched its third raid against Berlin the next day, it was pushing its luck too far. Some 20 Lancasters were lost, of 366 sent out, while poor weather reduced the effectiveness of the bombing. Crews reported much heavier flak and nightfighter defences, indicating that the Luftwaffe had already realised that Berlin had become the primary target in a new bombing offensive. A further 2000 houses were destroyed, and another 1400-1500 Berliners were killed.

When German controllers found their orders being countermanded by a German voice broadcast from England, they switched to a female controller to relay the all-important 'running commentary'. To their astonishment, the British immediately followed with their own German female voice, who ordered the nightfighters to land immediately due to the fog forming at their bases!

Three new Lancaster units, Nos 432, 463 and 550 Sqns, were involved in the fourth raid on 26/27 November – 28 Lancasters failed to return of the 443 despatched, and 14 more crashed in England. The raid caused further damage, despite the Pathfinders marking an area about seven miles north-west of the city centre. Berlin Zoo was hit again, and many large and dangerous animals escaped, roaming the streets and complicating the task of the rescue workers and defenders. This fourth attack brought Berlin's total death toll in November to 4330, with 104,613 homes destroyed and 417,665 people being 'bombed out'.

After a series of minor operations, Bomber Command returned to Berlin on 2/3 December with 425 Lancasters, 18 Mosquitos and 15 Halifaxes. These were scattered by very heavy winds, and 37 Lancasters failed to return, together with two Halifaxes and a single Mosquito. The losses included five Lancasters from the 25 sortied by No 460 Sqn, two of which had been carrying war correspondents from the *Daily*

HELLZAPOPPIN! was almost certainly W4198/QR-H of No 61 Sqn. Seen here with 71 missions recorded, the aircraft was lost on its 75th operation, against Berlin, on 26/27 November 1943, along with Plt Off A J Eaves and his seven-man crew. The 4000-lb 'Cookie' being manoeuvred into place bears a self-explanatory message, which has clearly been applied with great care and skill, probably for the benefit of attendant press photographers *(via Bruce Robertson)*

Mail and the *Sydney Sun* – both reporters were killed. Berlin was poorly marked, and bombing was scattered and damage light. Some 36 Berliners were killed.

The next day, a massive force of 307 Lancasters and 220 Halifaxes appeared on German radar screens heading straight for Berlin. These then veered off and attacked Leipzig, which was virtually undefended, and the mass of fighters sent aloft to defend Berlin found only a handful of evasive diversionary Mosquitos. Only about three aircraft were lost in the target area (where damage was heavy), but many bombers strayed close to Frankfurt on the return, and 15 Halifaxes and nine Lancasters failed to return.

Another attack against Berlin was undertaken on 16/17 December, involving 483 Lancasters and 15 Mosquitos. Despite cloud cover marking was accurate and damage was heavy, with about 700 Berliners being killed. The proportion of Berlin's accommodation rendered unusable rose to 25 per cent, and severe damage had been inflicted on the city's rail network. Some 25 Lancasters were lost during the mission, and 29 more were lost in crashes or were abandoned by their crews when they encountered low cloud and fog at their bases. No 97 Sqn alone lost seven aircraft in the crashes, and Bomber Command as a whole lost 148 men killed, 39 injured and six presumed lost at sea.

After a further series of minor operations, Bomber Command's next big raid (with 390 Lancasters and 257 Halifaxes) was made against Frankfurt on 20/21 December. Damage was heavy, but creepback and a German decoy fire led to many bombs being dropped in residential areas rather than in the industrial areas being targeted. 14 Lancasters and 27 Halifaxes failed to return.

Berlin was re-visited again on 23/24 December by seven Halifaxes, eight Mosquitos and 364 Lancasters. 'Only' 16 Lancasters were lost, although marking of the cloud-covered city was poor and damage was correspondingly light. Bomber Command thought that it did better on 29/30 December, when the city was re-visited by 457 Lancasters and 252 Halifaxes, but German records report that the attack was no more effective. Eleven Lancasters and nine Halifaxes failed to return.

Another 28 Lancasters fell on 1/2 January 1944, during another relatively ineffective raid on the German capital, this time by 421 Lancasters. Another 27 failed to return the next night (of 362 despatched) from a mission which resulted in 'scattered bombing' according to Berlin records. Though losses on these two nights were similar, the way in which they were inflicted was not. On 1/2 January the defences were relatively ineffective over Berlin itself (where two aircraft were downed by fighters and two by flak), whereas the following night most of the losses were inflicted by nightfighters in the target area itself.

The crew of No IX Sqn's W4964 were too good for the propaganda photographers to miss, with a pilot from Ipswich, a bomb aimer from Winnipeg, a W/Op from Melbourne, a flight engineer from Hornsey and gunners from Scotland, Chichester and New York. Such mixed crews were by no means unusual within Bomber Command. Seen here after a successful attack on Stettin on 6 January 1944, W4964 *Johnny Walker* completed at least seven missions against Berlin, and survived the war with a bomb log which recorded 106 operations (all with No IX Sqn). The bomber served as a Ground Instructional airframe from November 1944 until struck off charge in 1949 *(via Bruce Robertson)*

2/3 January was a particularly difficult night for the Pathfinders, who lost ten aircraft, five of them from No 156 Sqn.

Berlin received only a diversionary attack by Mosquitos on 5/6 January, with 348 Lancasters and ten Halifaxes instead attacking Stettin. Sixteen bombers were lost, 14 of them Lancasters, but damage to the town in its first major raid since 1941 was heavy. Brunswick suffered its first raid of the war on 14/15 January, when it came under attack by 496 Lancasters and a pair of Halifaxes – 38 Lancasters were shot down, 11 of them Pathfinders, and the attack was virtually ineffective, destroying only ten houses and killing just 14 civilians.

Things went equally badly on 20/21 January, when 495 Lancasters and 264 Halifaxes managed to miss Berlin altogether, but lost 22 Halifaxes and 13 Lancasters in the process. One Halifax unit, No 102 Sqn, lost five of its sixteen aircraft, with two more crashing in England on return. Four more were lost the next night during an equally ineffective attack against Magdeburg by 421 Lancasters and 224 Halifaxes. They were among 35 Halifaxes and 22 Lancasters that failed to return that night.

Berlin was attacked by 515 Lancasters on 27/28 January, and 33 bombers were lost. A raid by 432 Lancasters and 241 Halifaxes followed on 28/29 January, and this time 26 Halifaxes and 20 Lancasters were lost. At last the cloud cover over Berlin was partly broken, and bombing accuracy was correspondingly higher during this mission. Bomber Command assessed this as its most concentrated attack of the campaign, a claim partly borne out by German records. Some 180,000 Berliners were 'bombed out' that night, and many important buildings were damaged.

At least 1000 Berliners are believed to have perished on the last night of the month, during a major attack by 440 Lancasters and 82 Halifaxes. Bomber Command again relied completely on sky marking, bombing through solid cloud cover and this time achieving a degree of concentration by most attacking aircraft, although 79 nearby towns and villages also suffered damage. 32 Lancasters were lost, along with a single Halifax.

By the end of January 14 large raids had consumed 7403 sorties and cost Bomber Command 384 aircraft. Berlin had, for its part, suffered heavy damage and horrifying casualties, but was far from the state of collapse expected by Harris when he launched the campaign.

The next attack against Berlin, on 15/16 February, broke many records. The force of 561 Lancasters, 314 Halifaxes and 16 Mosquitos was bigger than the previous record of 826 despatched against Dortmund in May 1943, and the total bomb tonnage of 2642 tons also set a record. 26 Lancasters and 17 Halifaxes were lost, but damage to the city was heavy, removing 1000 houses and 526 temporary barracks from the housing stock and killing 320 people. Many regard the 15/16 February attack as marking the end of the Battle of Berlin, since the city would now be ignored for more than a month.

The next major attack was targeted against Leipzig, Bomber Command despatching 561 Lancasters and 255 Halifaxes, as well as the usual handful of Mosquitos. The Bomber Stream came under virtually constant attack by enemy fighters, and many aircraft arrived at the target early, forcing them to orbit while they waited for the Pathfinders to arrive. Four were lost in collisions and 20 more were shot down by flak – 44 Lancasters and 34 Halifaxes were lost.

Left and below
No 50 Sqn's ED470/VN-O visited Berlin on at least three occasions and survived the damage shown here, sustained during a mission to Leipzig. The aircraft is believed to have passed to No 61 Sqn, with whom it was lost on 23 September 1944. The photo below shows Flt Sgt E T McLeod posing alongside his flak-damaged tail turret (both via Bruce Robertson)

When early returns were excluded, the Halifax loss rate reached a staggering 14.9 per cent, and this was enough for Harris to permanently withdraw the B II and B V from Main Force operations over Germany. Merlin-powered Halifaxes continued to be used for mining, and by a single Pathfinder squadron, whilst the newer B III remained fully committed to the offensive. The Halifax B III even re-equipped a single Lancaster unit during February 1944 when No 432 Sqn converted from the Lancaster B II to the Halifax within No 6 Group.

Three further units would receive Lancasters during the following month, with the last Halifax squadron in No 8 Group (No 35 Sqn) converting to the Avro bomber and No 3 Group gaining a second Lancaster unit (following No 115, which had converted one year earlier) in the form of No 75 Sqn at Mepal, in Cambridgeshire. The Pathfinders also gained another new Lancaster unit with the formation of No 635 Sqn at Downham Market.

Stuttgart was attacked on 20/21 February, but heavy cloud cover led to scattered bombing. The city was quite badly damaged, however, and Bomber Command escaped with the loss of only seven Lancasters and two Halifaxes of 460 and 126 despatched, respectively.

After the massive raid by 266 USAAF B-17s on 24 February, Schweinfurt was attacked by 11 Mosquitos, 554 Lancasters and 169 Halifaxes on 24/25 February. These were split into two waves of 392 and 342 aircraft, which attacked with a two-hour interval. The first wave

Flt Sgt E J Wilkie and Plt Off J M Hollingsworth of No 426 'Thunderbird' Sqn perch on a highly decorated 8000-lb bomb, flanked by Victory Bonds posters, at Linton-on-Ouse, in North Yorkshire, on 21 February 1944 (via Bruce Robertson)

Heavy snow was just another obstacle for Bomber Command's hard pressed air- and groundcrews, but every effort was made to clear taxiways and runways to allow operations to continue. This photograph was taken in early March 1944 (via Phil Jarrett)

suffered a 5.6 per cent loss rate while the second wave lost only 3.2 per cent, and only four of the eleven aircraft lost in the second wave were downed by enemy fighters. Of 33 aircraft lost, 26 were Lancasters.

The most effective attack mounted during February was made against Augsburg on 25/26 February. Effective diversions reduced losses to 16 Lancasters and five Halifaxes, of 461 and 123 despatched, respectively, while clear weather conditions allowed an exceptionally accurate attack. Augsburg's beautiful centre was entirely destroyed, and very cold temperatures hampered the fire fighting operations, with the river and many water hoses having frozen. Bombing was, ironically, so concentrated that there was relatively little damage to the modern outskirts of Augsburg, where most industry was concentrated.

Stuttgart was hit almost as hard on 1/2 March, when only four Lancasters (of 415) and one Halifax (of 129) were lost. Thick cloud hampered the German nightfighters more than the bombers, which hit the town's historic centre especially hard.

March saw the beginnings of major attacks against French targets, often by Mosquitos and Halifaxes alone. 56 Lancasters participated (alongside 242 Halifaxes) in the attack against railway yards at Le Mans on 7/8 March, and 44 No 5 Group Lancasters mounted a small operation against the aircraft factory at Marignane, near Marseilles, on 9/10 March, one of a succession of minor 'Lancaster only' attacks.

The next German target to be hit was again Stuttgart, on 15/16 March, which cost Bomber Command 27 Lancasters (of 617 despatched) and 10 Halifaxes (of 230). Most of the bombing fell outside the city.

Frankfurt was Bomber Command's next target, attracting attacks on 18/19 and 22/23 March – the same city was also attacked by the USAAF by day on 24 March, causing further damage. The first raid was by 846 aircraft (620 Lancasters, 209 Halifaxes and 17 Mosquitos) and caused heavy damage and considerable casualties, for the loss of only ten Lancasters and 12 Halifaxes. The second attack was even more devastating, killing nearly 1000 people and causing immense damage and destruction. Losses were heavier, too, with 26 of the 620 Lancasters failing to return and seven of the 184 Halifaxes.

27

Berlin suffered its last major attack of the war (although Mosquitos would continue to make small scale attacks) on 24/25 March 1944. This involved 811 aircraft (577 Lancasters, 216 Halifaxes and 18 Mosquitos), which suffered an 8.9 per cent loss rate, mainly to flak. A powerful wind blew the Bomber Stream south and played havoc with the PFF's ability to mark the target, resulting in bombs being widely scattered – the main concentration of bombs fell in the south-western districts. 44 Lancasters and 28 Halifaxes failed to return, and the total number of aircrew lost far exceeded the 150 Germans killed in the attack.

The Battle of Berlin had failed. But while it had not resulted in the collapse predicted by Harris, nor had the campaign been a complete defeat, and many lessons had been learned which would improve Bomber Command's effectiveness for the rest of the war.

Improved navigational accuracy and the withdrawal of older, slower types allowed the bomber stream to be compressed, covering a 70-mile strip instead of the 300 miles common in 1942. This meant that 800 aircraft could 'feed through' the target in only about 20 minutes, minimising their exposure to enemy defences.

Many of the Halifaxes and Stirlings dropped from Main Force raids were used to mount massive diversionary operations, using prodigious quantities of 'Window' to simulate a Main Force attack, but actually attacking coastal targets or minelaying.

But losses remained unsustainably high, and bomber aircrew morale suffered accordingly. During the battle many bomber aircrew went straight from training units to squadrons on which a raid on Berlin marked their introduction to operations. These morale problems had a direct impact on operations, too. An unwillingness among some crews to press through the heaviest defences led to a growing phenomenon of 'creepback', as aircraft dropped their bombs early and the bombing extended back into the countryside away from the aim point.

In No 1 Group, where there was the greatest enthusiasm for loading the aircraft with ever heavier bombloads, some crews reacted by jettisoning their bombs over the North Sea. On some nights, when No 1 Group was flying, the course of the bomber stream was marked by a series of explosions far below, and the problem became serious enough for Bomber Command to issue orders banning this practice.

With a bomb log totalling 65 missions, including three attacks on Italian targets (marked by ice cream cones!) *DANTE'S DAUGHTER* (ED731/AS-T2) of No 166 Sqn failed to return from Berlin on 24/25 March 1944 whilst being flown by Flg Off T L Teasdale RCAF and his crew. An ex-No 103 Sqn machine, ED731 was on its 12th mission to the German capital when it was shot down *(via Bruce Robertson)*

Seen here taxying at Skellingthorpe, in Lincolnshire, DV397/QR-W of No 61 Sqn was another bomber lost on the 24/25 March 1944 Berlin raid – it had survived identical missions three times before. No fewer than 72 aircraft were lost on this night, 44 of them Lancasters. No 61 Sqn flew 4546 sorties with the Avro bomber, losing 116 aircraft in the process. During February, March and the first half of April 1944, the unit operated from Coningsby, again in Lincolnshire *(via Bruce Robertson)*

Nearly 400 Bomber Command aircraft were lost in direct raids against Berlin itself, and more were downed in diversionary raids and other attacks mounted during the period. Sixteen major attacks were made against Berlin (totalling 9111 sorties), with 208 further sorties flown on other nights.

Harris had originally conceived his all-out assault on Berlin as including the US Eighth Air Force, operating under his command, by night, in a fully integrated campaign, although such participation was impossible. The USAAF was not about to let its premier combat unit in Europe come under 'foreign' command, even temporarily, while even had it been willing to do so, its crews were not trained for night bombing.

Following the horrifying losses of February's 'Big Week' (when the USAAF lost more than 400 aircraft in 3300 sorties) the 'Mighty Eighth' barely paused to re-group before turning its attentions to what many of its aircrew referred to as the 'Big B' – Berlin. Berlin was regarded as something of a 'prestige target', and many aircrew looked forward to adding it to their mission tally. Few realised how difficult and dangerous a target it would turn out to be, however. With the P-51 now in service in large numbers, USAAF bombers could be escorted 'all the way' to Berlin, and a first abortive attack on the German capital was attempted on 3 March. B-17s finally reached and attacked Berlin the following day during another mission which was supposed to have been aborted – one wing failed to receive a weather recall!

Two days later, the Eighth attacked again with 800 bombers and nearly as many escort fighters, but the defences (now alerted to the possibility of daylight attacks) were waiting, and inflicted heavy losses on the Americans. An alert fighter controller realised that a division in the middle of the stream was unescorted, and concentrated fighter efforts against this formation. In total, 69 bombers were shot down, and 105 were severely damaged. The 350th BS alone lost ten aircraft, and other units were similarly badly mauled. Bombing accuracy was understandably poor.

Gen James Doolittle launched 600 bombers against Berlin again on 8 March, achieving greater accuracy, but at a cost of 37 more of his bombers. Two smaller raids followed during the remainder of March.

The effects of the day and night bombing on Berlin were relatively insignificant, although there was considerable damage to the city and its infrastructure. But despite the bombing, Berlin's war production actually increased during the period, and although fully one fifth of the city's population was made homeless, there was little crisis of civilian morale, and utilities and services continued to function.

The bombing may have brought it home to the population that the war was entering a new (and perhaps even final phase), and may have shaken public confidence in the Nazi Party's ability to defend the country, if not in Hitler's leadership. Hitler himself was unmoved by the bombing, which did not shake his commitment to putting maximum effort into offensive and not defensive weapons. It would be fanciful to give too much credence to suggestions that the bombing motivated the July plotters against Hitler, or that it led them to believe that their plot would gain widespread support.

In fact, like the Londoners before them, Berliners displayed something of a 'Blitz spirit', and suffered little 'shock effect' even when the battle began. Berlin had, after all, been attacked many times before. There was a useful effect on the enemy's workforce, however, with bombing inevitably producing apathy and nervous exhaustion, and an absenteeism rate which would eventually soar to an average of 23.5 days per worker per year by mid 1944. Moreover, the destruction caused by bombing diverted labour to repair and restoration work, while some industrial production capacity had to supply bombed-out and evacuated families with the essential goods they left behind in their shattered dwellings.

Overall, Bomber Command's offensive also tied up large numbers of men in the flak arm and fighter defences, and diverted guns and fighter aircraft from the fronts. The attacks also prompted Hitler to divert massive resources to his 'Vengeance' weapons, further eroding the Wehrmacht's ability to fight the 'real war'. It has been estimated, for example, that the V2 programme consumed as much money, manpower and materials as 24,000 fighter aircraft, and achieved almost nothing.

The effect on Bomber Command was probably more serious than the effect on the German economy, however. Over the whole period, losses averaged 5.4 per cent, but this masked a growing loss rate as the defences (and especially the flak arm) became progressively more effective. The first attack in December 1943 suffered an 8.7 per cent loss rate, while the final attack in March 1944 suffered 9.1 per cent losses. This was plainly unsustainable, and Harris was forced to abandon his offensive against the German capital.

If the failure of the offensive against Berlin undermined confidence in Bomber Command, another area attack against a prominent German city would have an even more shocking effect. The attack against Nuremberg on 30 March 1944 would deal Bomber Command its heaviest defeat of the war, with a shocking 13.6 per cent casualty rate, while inflicting little damage on the target itself.

More than a dozen Lancaster noses are seen lined up for repair at Bracebridge Heath, in Lincolnshire. Due to its close proximity to numerous Bomber Command airfields in the 'bomber county', this facility was kept busy patching up battle-damaged bombers and hastily returning them to operations. The Battle of Berlin placed particular strain on the factories and repair facilities, generating a huge requirement for replacement aircraft. The nose section nearest to the camera is part of B III JB351 (note the serial chalked below the cockpit), formerly of No 83 Sqn. Reissued to No 61 Sqn upon its departure from Bracebridge Heath, this aircraft was subsequently damaged again on 22 June 1944 by a German nightfighter, and although it limped back to base, the bomber was declared uneconomic to repair and struck off charge
(via Bruce Robertson)

NUREMBERG

The final attack on Berlin on 24/25 March 1944 was followed by a devastatingly effective mission to Essen, which caught the Luftwaffe almost entirely by surprise, and only six of 476 Lancasters and three of 207 Halifaxes failed to return. The next target would be even more unexpected, at least for the bomber crews.

Nuremberg was an important symbolic target for the RAF, not least because of its close associations with the early rise of Nazism, and for the grandiose rallies held there before the war. Many viewed the city as the cradle of Nazism, and as its shrine. This alone made it worth attacking, and the city's status as a major industrial centre only heightened its appeal. Nuremberg lay further east and further south than most of Bomber Command's targets, however, with only towns like Augsburg and Munich being harder to reach for the RAF 'heavies'.

Distance alone afforded Nuremberg a degree of protection, and some therefore expected it to be relatively lightly defended, and for it to be possible to take advantage of the element of surprise when attacking the city. It is probably true that a well-planned and well-executed attack could have succeeded, but unfortunately the Bomber Command mission mounted on the night of 30/31 March 1944 was neither.

The cancellation of a raid on Brunswick on 29/30 March enabled many squadrons to commit a signficant number of their aircraft to the Nuremburg operation, even though a 'Maximum Effort' had not been ordered. Many of the crews, however, lacked the experience to handle such a long range attack – indeed, 100 crews had flown six ops or less, and 18 crews were flying their first. Eight of the latter would fail to return, and losses among the other inexperienced crews were scarcely any lighter.

The route chosen went down into Belgium, before turning east to fly between the heavily defended areas of the Ruhr and Frankfurt, dog-legging south to Nuremberg, then continuing in this direction before finally turning west to escape over northern France. No one was happy about the plan. Nos 1, 4 and 6 Groups were unhappy about the weather forecast, which promised to leave their aircraft exposed, flying virtually all the way in full moonlight and with no cloud cover, except in the vital

Photographed in January 1944, B I W4113 was another long-lived Lancaster, serving with No 49 Sqn until early 1942, when it joined No 156. After the Nuremberg raid, the aircraft eventually transferred to No 1661 CU as GP-J. Following service with a number of training units, the bomber became a Ground Instructional airframe in December 1944 *(via Phil Jarrett)*

target area, where there promised to be unbroken cloud at low level, but still with no high level cloud cover. No 1 Group in particular queried the wisdom of launching the raid without such cloud cover. No 100 Group did not like the route either, because it took the bomber stream between two major assembly beacons used by enemy nightfighters, but it was judged to be too late to change the route.

While the Germans had no knowledge as to the target of the raid, they were soon aware that a major attack was being planned, as bombers flew air tests in preparation for the night's operations, and later as the Pathfinders took off and turned on their H₂S radar sets. All PFF Lancasters were by then equipped with H$_2$S, along with about 128 Main Force aircraft. Confirmation was supplied as the bombers formed up over East Anglia, with the Wassermann radar near Ostend detecting the raiders.

The first of 569 Lancasters and 212 Halifaxes took off at 2216 hrs and continued to Charleroi, where they dog-legged east. Stronger than forecast winds and heavy jamming of *Gee* began to affect the bomber stream, with aircraft straying north of their intended track. Meanwhile, the northern force's 49 Halifaxes were recognised as a diversion as they descended to begin mining, and the Luftwaffe nightfighters remained at readiness. The Main Force was clearly heading for a more southerly target than Berlin or Hamburg. Thus, when scrambled, the nightfighters were ordered to assemble at Beacons *Otto* (near Köln) and *Ida* (south of the Ruhr). This covered both of what the Germans considered to be the prime targets, placing them either side of the bombers' planned track.

A spoof raid by Mosquitos against Aachen was ignored as it branched north from the Main Force, as was another targeted at Köln and a final spoof feinting towards Kassel. Running battles between nightfighters and bombers began even as the first Lancasters crossed the Belgian border, and at least 60 bombers fell before the bomber stream reached the dog-leg south.

Many crews had hitherto believed British propaganda which ascribed the huge explosions sometimes seen

A veteran of five missions to Berlin, B III LM418 was No 619 Sqn's only casualty at Nuremberg, being destroyed in a crash-landing at Woodbridge, in Suffolk, after losing two engines to a prowling nightfighter. Although the aircraft was a total loss, Sgt J Parker's landing was good enough to save the lives of his crew *(via Francis K Mason)*

No 463 Sqn Lancaster B I LL847 survived the Nuremberg raid, along with 17 other aircraft despatched by the RAAF's third Lancaster unit. Only Nos 35, 83 and 405 Sqns (all Pathfinder units) and Nos XV, 100, 463 and 626 Sqns escaped loss at Nuremberg of the 34 Lancaster units participating. The slaughter was especially intense for the least experienced crews, with eight of 18 first mission crews failing to return. LL847 was subsequently lost on the 17/18 December 1944 mission to Munich. The artwork beneath the bomber's cockpit features two 'Diggers' playing 'Two Up', a famous Australian gambling game that was popular amongst the troops *(via Francis K Mason)*

as being caused by a pyrotechnic 'scarecrow' fired by the Germans to undermine morale, but it soon became clear that these 'scarecrows' were actually British bombers exploding as their bombs 'cooked off'. The German fighter pilots found themselves in an extremely 'target-rich' environment, and many scored several victories. Probably the most successful was 58-kill ace Oberleutnant Martin Becker of I./NJG 4, based at Finthen, near Mainz, who found himself in the bomber stream even as he climbed towards beacon *Ida*. Within 30 minutes he had downed three Lancasters and three Halifaxes, before landing back at Finthen to rearm and refuel. He downed another Halifax during his second sortie of the night. 'Tino' Becker was known for his multiple-kill hauls, claiming six bombers on 23 March 1944 and nine on 14 March 1945. He survived the war.

Many of the nightfighters' victims fell prey to German aircraft equipped with the new upward-firing *Schräge Musik* cannon, and several bomber crews escaped by parachute. When using *Schräge Musik*, the wise fighter pilot aimed for the bomber's fuel tanks rather than the bomb-bay, since an immediate explosion would often risk destroying hunter along with the hunted, especially if a 'Cookie' were being carried. This sometimes gave bomber aircrew time to escape by parachute.

By the time they were abeam the Ruhr, the bombers were strung out across a 40-mile front, and those Lancasters still flying at their briefed altitude were trailing phosphorescent contrails. The usual running commentary was virtually superfluous, so the 26 ABC-equipped Lancasters despatched by No 101 Sqn had little to do.

Nuremberg should have been marked by nine Mosquitos using 500-lb bombs, 'Window' and green TIs, followed five minutes later by 24 Lancasters dropping green TIs and hooded flares, and finally by 62 Lancaster 'supporters' dropping 4000-lb bombs and 'Window'. This should have 'turned night into day' over Nuremberg, and blinded the city's radar-directed flak batteries. These were to be followed by six low-level Lancasters, precisely aiming 60 mixed green and red TIs.

The Main Force bombers had been due to attack at the rate of 57 per minute (dropping 180 tons per minute), with the whole force flowing through the target in only 12 minutes.

The seven-man crew of No 50 Sqn's 'T-for-Tommy' pose in front of their aircraft. This unit lost three aircraft to enemy action at Nuremberg, and one more crashed on landing, of the 19 sent out. No 61 Sqn (temporarily based at Coningsby, but usually permanently stationed at Skellingthorpe) lost another two *(via Phil Jarrett)*

These plans had already come under pressure as a result of the heavy losses (75 combat losses and about 55 aborts) and poor navigation, but weather conditions would now further spoil Bomber Command's night.

Nuremberg was entirely obscured by a thick belt of cloud stretching up to 10,000 ft or more, and the handful of emergency sky markers dropped by the most accurate Pathfinders were soon swallowed up. There was no Master Bomber to direct the Main Force to bomb on sky markers, and only a small proportion of bombers bombed anywhere near Nuremberg, with the small town of Lauf, ten miles east, receiving the bulk of the bombs dropped in the target area.

Many of the aircraft which had straggled north of their planned track reached a large target, clear of cloud, just when they expected to see Nuremberg. This group was led by a PFF Mosquito, which confidently unloaded its 500-lb bombs and green TIs bang on time, and was followed by six Lancaster supporters and two Pathfinder 'backers up'. Some 70 Lancasters and 29 Halifaxes attacked this well-marked target with great accuracy, although unfortunately it turned out to be Schweinfurt.

More Lancasters and Halifaxes were scythed down as they straggled home, with ten aircraft being destroyed in crashes and forced landings in England. A total of 96 aircraft were lost, including 78 to enemy night-fighters. The carnage could have been even worse had the single-engined *Wilde Sau* aircraft not been held on the ground in anticipation of an attack on Berlin. 55 Lancasters were lost, five were downed by flak and seven crashed. One more was lost in a collision with a Halifax, and one Lancaster simply failed to return. This represented 12.13 per cent of the aircraft despatched. The Halifax loss rate was even higher.

Bomber Command lost 96 aircraft in the Nuremberg raid (10.1 per cent of the force despatched, and Bomber Command's worst loss of the war), including 64 Lancasters. In return it killed just 69 civilians in Nuremberg and the surrounding villages. About 13 aircraft were lost on the return journey, and ten were written off in England in crashes and forced landings. This particular Lancaster is being hoisted up onto a tractor unit to facilitate its removal from a Lincolnshire field post-Nuremberg (via Phil Jarrett)

COLOUR PLATES

1
Lancaster B I LM220/WS-Y of No IX Sqn, Bardney, 1944

2
Lancaster B I RA530/DX-Y of No 57 Sqn, East Kirkby, early 1945

3
Lancaster B I EE176/QR-M of No 61 Sqn, Skellingthorpe, 1945

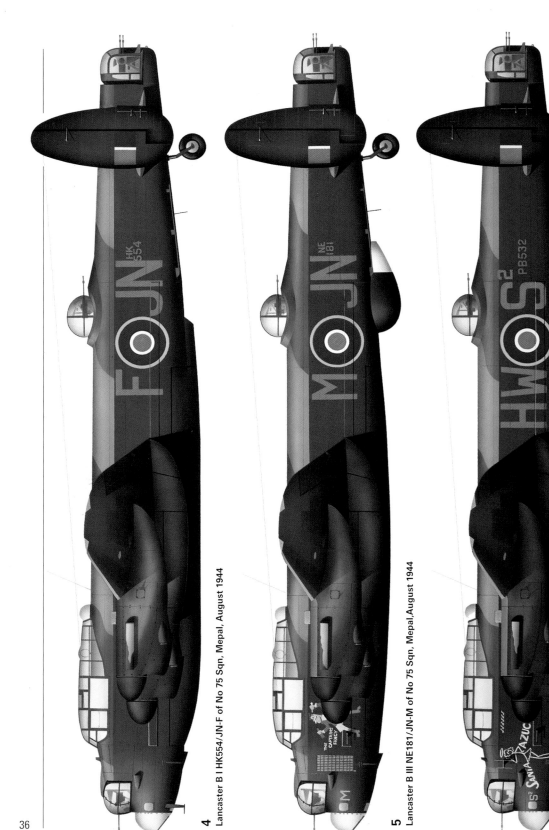

4
Lancaster B I HK554/JN-F of No 75 Sqn, Mepal, August 1944

5
Lancaster B III NE181/JN-M of No 75 Sqn, Mepal, August 1944

6
Lancaster B III PB532/HW-S² of No 100 Sqn, Elsham Wolds, April 1945

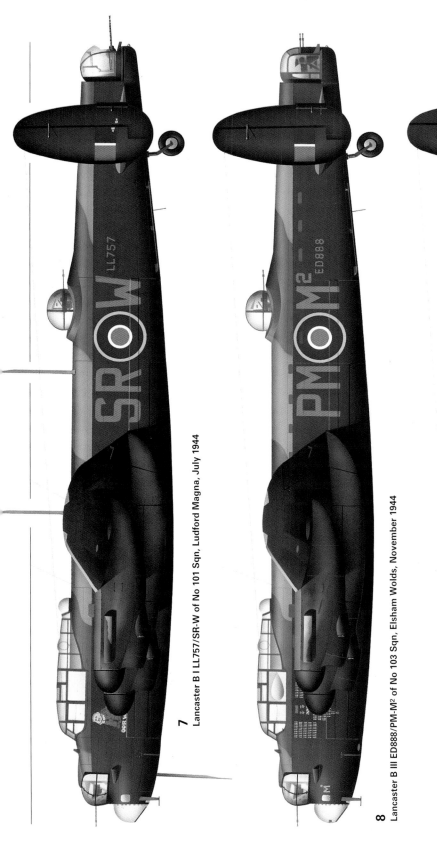

7

Lancaster B I LL757/SR-W of No 101 Sqn, Ludford Magna, July 1944

8

Lancaster B III ED888/PM-M² of No 103 Sqn, Elsham Wolds, November 1944

9

Lancaster B III JB663/ZN-A of No 106 Sqn, Metheringham, 6 November 1944

10
Lancaster B III PB509/OJ-C of No 149 Sqn, Methwold, early 1945

11
Lancaster B III ME812/AS-F of No 166 Sqn, Kirmington, June 1944

12
Lancaster B III PB480/TC-G^2 of No 170 Sqn, Hemswell, March 1945

13

Lancaster B III ND758/A4-A of No 195 Sqn, Witchford, October 1944

14

Lancaster B II LL725/EQ-Z of No 408 Sqn, Linton-on-Ouse, 24 April 1944

15

Lancaster B X KB732/VR-X of No 419 Sqn, Middleton St George, 1945

16
Lancaster B I NG347/QB-P of No 424 Sqn, Skipton on Swale, 1945

17
Lancaster B X KB848/NA-G of No 428 Sqn, Middleton St George, May 1945

18
Lancaster B X KB864/NA-S of No 428 Sqn, Middleton St George, May 1945

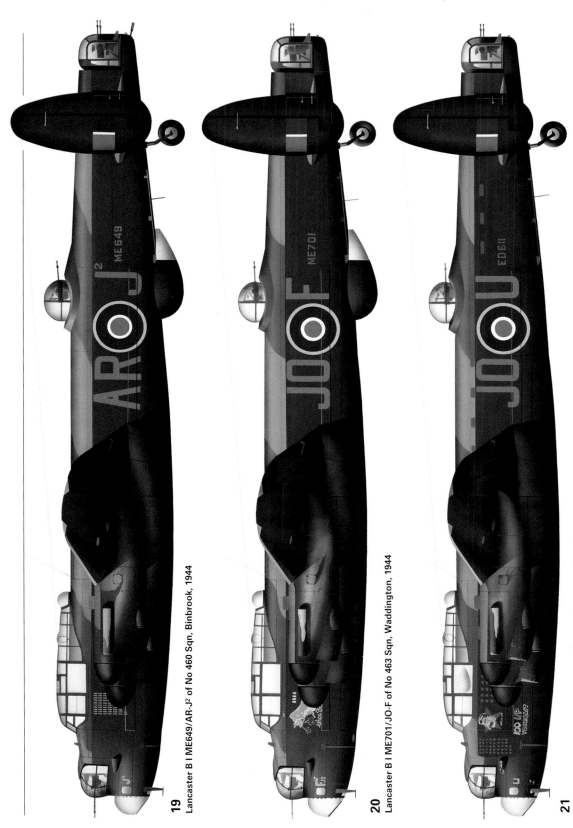

19

Lancaster B I ME649/AR-J[2] of No 460 Sqn, Binbrook, 1944

20

Lancaster B I ME701/JO-F of No 463 Sqn, Waddington, 1944

21

Lancaster B III ED611/JO-U of No 463 Sqn, Waddington, June 1944

41

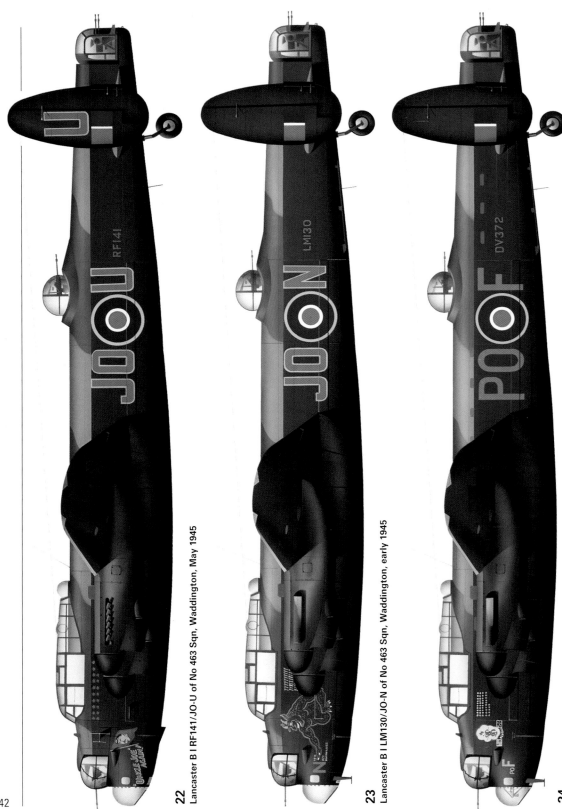

22
Lancaster B I RF141/JO-U of No 463 Sqn, Waddington, May 1945

23
Lancaster B I LM130/JO-N of No 463 Sqn, Waddington, early 1945

24
Lancaster B I DV372/PO-F of No 467 Sqn, Waddington, October 1944

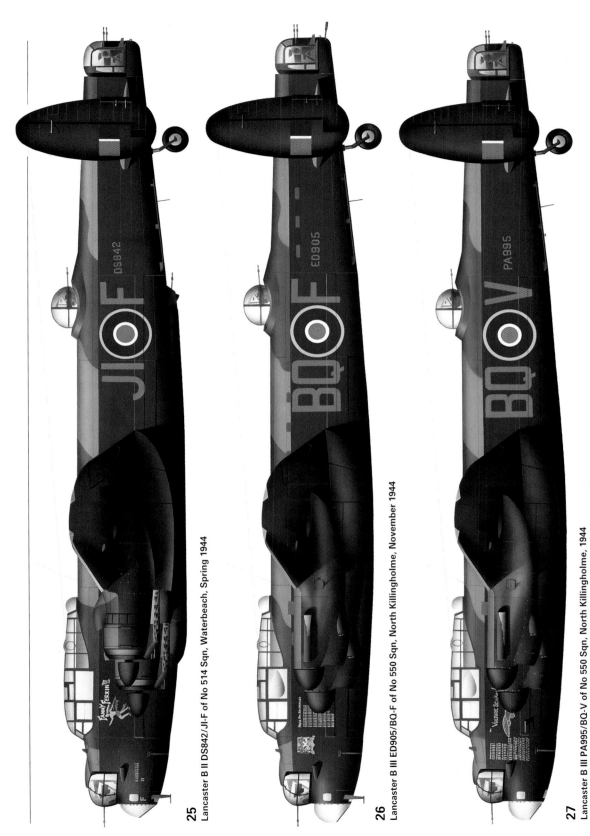

25
Lancaster B II DS842/JI-F of No 514 Sqn, Waterbeach, Spring 1944

26
Lancaster B III ED905/BQ-F of No 550 Sqn, North Killingholme, November 1944

27
Lancaster B III PA995/BQ-V of No 550 Sqn, North Killingholme, 1944

28 Lancaster B I LM227/UL-I of No 576 Sqn, Elsham Wolds, 1945

29 Lancaster B I DV385/KC-A of No 617 Sqn, Woodhall Spa, mid 1944

30 Lancaster B I ED763/KC-Z of No 617 Sqn, Woodhall Spa, October 1944

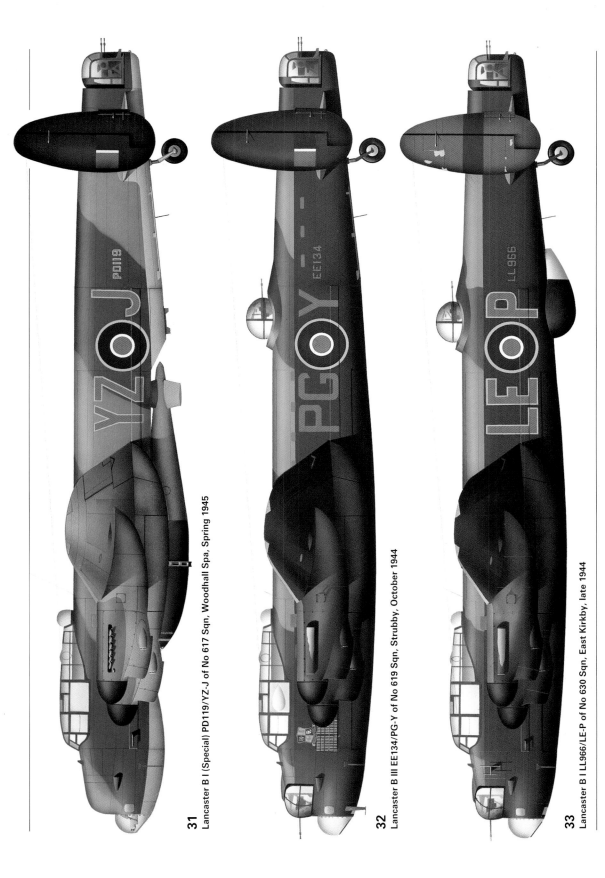

31

Lancaster B I (Special) PD119/YZ-J of No 617 Sqn, Woodhall Spa, Spring 1945

32

Lancaster B III EE134/PG-Y of No 619 Sqn, Strubby, October 1944

33

Lancaster B I LL966/LE-P of No 630 Sqn, East Kirkby, late 1944

D-DAY/TACTICAL

'Bomber' Harris had an entirely unrealistic view of the overall significance and importance of Bomber Command's role, predicting in mid 1942 that it could win the war alone, with a continental land campaign having no use except for 'mopping up' and describing the 'entirely defensive' Coastal Command as 'merely an obstacle to victory'.

Harris's unwillingness to see 'his' heavy bombers diverted to help Coastal Command was unhelpful, and undoubtedly gave Germany respite when it most needed it, and when the area bombing campaign was at its least effective and most costly. What might have happened had he diverted some of his bombers and crews to the Battle of the Atlantic, instead of squandering them in useless and inaccurate attacks on German industrial cities, is one of the war's great 'what if' questions. It did, however, have the effect of allowing Coastal Command to build up its own force of long range four-engined 'heavies', which numbered eight Liberator and four Halifax squadrons by mid-1944, together with further units operating the Warwick and Wellington, as well as the Sunderland and Catalina flying boats. Coastal Command even took 12 units of Beaufighters and Mosquitos.

And eventually, especially after D-Day, Harris did allow Bomber Command to be used against U-boat pens, harbours and enemy warships like the *Tirpitz*, with a high degree of success.

Even more surprisingly, Harris threw himself into providing air support for the continental land campaign with some energy and enthusiasm, supporting the invasion itself, and providing close air support and battlefield air interdiction for various ground offensives throughout the rest of the war.

Although Harris himself continued to expound the virtues of area bombing, and of directly targeting the enemy civilian populace, Bomber Command did become

With squadron codes repeated above the tailplane, PO-N (probably ND473) of No 467 Sqn blasts German defences during the run-up to Operation *Overlord* (via Phil Jarrett)

A survivor of the war was ND991/VN-P of No 50 Sqn, which was finally scrapped in 1947. Here, the aircraft waits to be loaded with some of the 500-lb bombs lying in the grass behind it in June 1944 (via Bruce Robertson)

Two veteran Lancasters prepare to taxi out at Skellingthorpe for a raid against Dugny, near Paris, on 10 August 1944. Nearest the camera is No 61 Sqn's ED860/QR-N with 118 ops under its belt, while ED588/VN-G (of No 50 Sqn) behind it had completed 116. A veteran of nine Berlin missions, ED860 was finally written off when it crashed on take-off from Skellingthorpe on 28 October 1944. ED588 successfully attacked Berlin on no less than 13 occasions, although it too ultimately failed to survive life in the frontline, being lost on the 29/30 August 1944 raid on Konigsburg
(via Francis K Mason)

steadily more accurate as the war progressed. In European weather, Bomber Command ended the war achieving better accuracy than the USAAF's supposedly precision bombing campaign. The USAAF was never as good at blind bombing as Bomber Command, and soon began what was effectively an area bombing offensive, albeit using what were euphemistically termed as railway marshalling yards as aim points in what were often area attacks against whole cities. Many doubt whether the USAAF could have pulled off the Peenemünde raid successfully, whereas

Flt Lt F R Davey and his crew pose in front of their No 625 Sqn Lancaster B III PB158/CF-G, nicknamed *GREEN GODDESS*. PB158 went missing on the 2 March 1945 daylight raid on Köln. No 625 Sqn had formed from No 100 Sqn's C Flight at Kelstern, in Lincolnshire, in October 1943
(via Francis K Mason)

A Lancaster bombs an oil depot near Bordeaux on 10 August 1944. 109 Lancasters and 101 Halifaxes, together with five Mosquitos, attacked oil targets at Bordeaux and La Pallice that night, all returning to base safely *(via Phil Jarrett)*

Bomber Command devastated the secret rocket establishment with exemplary precision.

The Peenemünde raid of August 1943 had conclusively demonstrated Bomber Command's ability to undertake precision bombing, and made it inevitable that the force would be placed under Gen Dwight Eisenhower's command to operate in support of Operation *Overlord*. Bomber Command was soon tasked with attacking a range of tactical targets in France.

Fortunately, Eisenhower's 'Air Commander', and second in command, Arthur Tedder, was himself a Strategic Bombing enthusiast who shared Harris's views on slogan warfare and panacea targets, and this took some of the sting out of Bomber Command's new temporary role, and helped to mollify Harris. The reaction of Bomber Command's own crews may also have helped Harris see the new campaign in a slightly better light, since they were enthusiastic in embracing an effort which was largely directed against military targets, and which promised to directly contribute to the invasion of occupied Europe.

Although there were no traditional all-out area attacks on German cities between 27/28 April (when Bomber Command attacked Friedrichshafen) and 23/24 July (when Kiel was bombed), the Command did mount a number of attacks against German cities containing oil refineries and important railway yards. After the Kiel attack, further raids were made against Bremen, Darmstadt, Frankfurt, Hamburg, Kiel once again, Königsberg, Munchengladbach, Rüsselsheim, Stettin and Stuttgart, before the 'heavies' 'officially' returned to Bomber Command control on 19 September.

Preparations for the Allied invasion of France began in earnest even as Bomber Command was fighting the Battle of Berlin. French railway targets at Amiens, Laon, Aulnoye, Courtrai and Vaires, along with other industrial targets, were attacked even before the ill-fated Nuremberg raid.

Bomber Command's effort was officially transferred to pre-invasion targets on 14 April 1944. The pace of attacks against railway targets in western Germany, Belgium and France rapidly picked up, with the Allies attempting to cut off enemy forces in Normandy from reinforcement by rail. Military camps, armament dumps, depots and factories also came

This anonymous Lancaster is dwarfed by the towering clouds of smoke caused by a massive raid, which has left the landscape pitted with craters *(via Phil Jarrett)*

ME703 of No 576 Sqn was not among the 42 Lancasters officially counted as 'lost' on 3/4 May 1944, after German nightfighters cut through the 346 bombers attacking a military camp close to the French village of Mailly. ME703 had lost one gunner killed and another missing in action, and despite the efforts of pilot Flg Off R R Reed, it never flew again. The operation had turned into a deadly farce when the Main Force Controller was unable to transmit the order to bomb (relayed from the Pathfinder leader, Leonard Cheshire) because his VHF radio set was wrongly tuned and was drowned out by an American Forces Broadcast *(via Bruce Robertson)*

under increasingly heavy attack. A similar level of effort was carried out to cut off the Pas de Calais from its reinforcements and supplies in furtherance of the deception that this latter area would actually be the target of the Anglo-American landings.

The campaign against invasion targets saw a further improvement in techniques and targeting accuracy, with an increase in the use of the Mosquito for target marking by both Nos 8 and 5 Groups. The latter group soon began to operate as an autonomous force once it had regained Nos 97 and 83 Sqns from the Pathfinders, and also its own Mosquito unit, No 627 Sqn, while No 617 gained a sizeable Mosquito flight specifically for target marking duties.

No 617 Sqn's charismatic CO, Wg Cdr Leonard Cheshire, pio-

With 27 mission marks already on its nose, B II DS729/EQ-V survived the Battle of Berlin and was not struck off until March 1945. Here, pilot Sqn Ldr Bill Russell of No 408 'Goose' Sqn talks to three of the fitters working on the aircraft's 'port inner' *(via Bruce Robertson)*

Though it is impossible to tell from this evocative silhouette, the Lancaster pictured here is (according to the Central Press caption writer) 'the veteran Lancaster bomber "S for Sugar" on her 87th officially recorded operation'. The caption writer went on to talk about the aircraft's 60 Pathfinder trips, and the award of a DSO and two DFCs to her various captains. This removes any doubt that the aircraft is anything other than R5868/PO-S of No 467 Sqn, now safely ensconced in the RAF Museum at Hendon. The aircraft's 87th op was flown against Sable on 6/7 May 1944 *(via Bruce Robertson)*

neered the technique on 5/6 April 1944 during an attack on an aircraft factory at Toulouse. The Mosquito's high speed gave him the chance to fly three passes over the target at low level before dropping his markers, which were then augmented by markers dropped by a pair of No 617 Sqn Lancasters. The 'ordinary' Lancaster squadrons of No 5 Group then bombed the target so successfully that the technique was immediately adopted. The result was that while the other groups had an average bombing error of 680 yards, No 5 Group's average was 380 yards.

By the time Bomber Command turned its attention to targets in France, the Merlin-engined Halifax had all but disappeared from the 22 frontline Halifax bomber units, and only Nos 346 and 428 Sqns still used the older version by D-Day. No 3 Group's re-equipment proceeded more slowly, however, and three units (Nos 90, 149 and 218 Sqns, plus No 199 Sqn of No 100 Group) were still operating the lumbering bombers. All the bomber Stirlings had retired by the end of August, however.

Bomber Command was already dominated by the Lancaster, with 40 squadrons on charge, most of them B Is and B IIIs. The Bomber Command Lancaster force still included some B IIs, however, and No 408 Sqn's radial-engined aircraft carried out a highly successful attack against coastal gun emplacements at Longues on the morning of D-Day itself. Low loss rates allowed the two remaining Lancaster B II units to serve on into the autumn of 1944, No 514 trading its Hercules-engined

The last anyone saw of Plt Off Andrew Mynarski, the mid-upper gunner of No 419 Sqn Lancaster KB726, was when he saluted his trapped colleague in the rear turret, before leaping to his death in burning clothes and parachute. Mynarski had sacrificed his own chances of survival in a vain attempt to free the rear gunner – who ironically survived when the aircraft crashed during a raid on Cambrai on 12/13 June 1944 *(via Bruce Robertson)*

aircraft for B Is and B IIIs between June and the end of September, while No 408 completed conversion to the Halifax B III in August 1944.

Attacks on coastal gun positions began during early May, while in the week leading up to the invasion the bombers attacked German radio listening stations, radar installations and radar jamming facilities, and dropped arms and equipment to the resistance.

On the night before D-Day, Bomber Command flew a record 1211 sorties, almost all of them in direct support of Operation *Overlord*, attacking enemy troops, gun positions, ammunition and oil dumps and road and rail communications. Enemy E-boats and other light offensive craft were also bombed in their French ports.

Sometimes the bombers flew close air support missions, attacking enemy positions that were within a few hundred yards of our own troops.

Even in the aftermath of the invasion, Bomber Command kept up a relentless pressure on German oil targets (especially in the Ruhr), and was diverted into a major offensive against the V1 flying bomb launch sites. Day bombing raids began again after D-Day, but since these were always within range of Allied escort fighters, losses were manageable.

A major raid against nine nightfighter airfields was mounted on 15 August by 1004 bombers (including 599 Lancasters) prior to the re-opening of a major night offensive against German cities. Enemy opposition was intense, although fighters had less warning and less time to react, and were also more vulnerable to Allied escort fighters, intruders and, when on the ground, prowling fighter-bombers. Many trace the start of the decline of the *Jagdwaffe* and *Nachtjagdwaffe* to the operations in Normandy.

The tactical bombing operations carried out in support of *Overlord* had conclusively demonstrated Bomber Command's ability to hit pinpoint

Five of the Lancasters which attacked the Trossy St Maxim flying bomb storage site on 3 August 1944 were lost during the operation. Some 601 Lancasters, 492 Halifaxes and 21 Mosquitos attacked three such targets that day *(via Francis K Mason)*

The oil depot at Pauillac after the 4 August attack by 288 Lancasters. They were accompanied by 27 *Serrate*-equipped Mosquito nightfighters (the first such use of Mosquitos so equipped) and suffered no losses *(via Phil Jarrett)*

targets with great precision. Up until D-Day, Harris had always argued that the area bombing of German cities was necessary because his force lacked the wherewithal to conduct more accurate attacks. Bomber Command's success (especially against the French transport system) during the run up to and aftermath of D-Day proved that this was untrue, and made it increasingly difficult for Harris to withstand demands for further attacks on precision targets.

On the same day as Lancasters attacked the oil depot at Pauillac, a smaller force revisited the Trossy St Maxim V1 storage site. Sqn Ldr I W Bazalgette won a posthumous VC during this latter attack after he pressed on and marked the target in a burning and mortally damaged No 635 Sqn Lancaster *(via Bruce Robertson)*

A Lancaster attacks targets east of Boulogne on 17 September 1944, prior to a planned attack by British and US Army troops. The demoralised German garrison surrendered soon after this raid *(via Francis K Mason)*

BIG BOMBS

Development of a new 12,000-lb High Capacity (HC) bomb for special purposes gave a reprieve to No 617 Sqn, which might otherwise have been disbanded following Operation *Chastise* (the 'Dams Raid') in May 1943. Replacement aircrew and aircraft were obtained and the squadron began training to return to operational status, beginning operations in mid July 1943. After an unsuccessful attack against two Italian power stations using conventional 1000-lb bombs (and landing in North Africa), the unit made a leaflet-dropping raid against Milan, before moving from Scampton to Coningsby on 30 August.

At the latter station, the mystified CO of No 617, Sqn Ldr G W Holden, was finally told of the unit's planned role as a specialised heavy attack squadron, employing the new 12,000-lb HC bomb initially against the vital Dortmund-Ems canal, which carried raw materials and manufactured goods (including pre-fabricated U-boat sections) between the Ruhr and Germany's northern ports. It was clear that breaching the canal's banks in a low lying area could empty it of water and cause massive flooding, but in such vulnerable locations the canal was heavily defended by flak guns, and previous attempts to attack it had been costly failures.

An abortive attempt on 14/15 September 1943 turned back while still over the North Sea, but cost the life of one of the surviving 'Dambusters', Sqn Ldr D J H Maltby. More 'Dambuster' survivors, including Plt Off L G Knight RAAF and his crew and five of Wg Cdr Guy Gibson's dams raid crew and the new CO, were lost the next night when the squadron reached the target but proved unable to cause any significant damage. The next night, the new acting CO, Sqn Ldr Mickey Martin, led an unsuccessful attack against the Antheor Viaduct in the south of France.

The first of the 'big bombs' used by Lancasters was the 12,000-lb HC device. This resembled three 4000-lb 'Cookies' bolted together, with a new annular tail unit, but was actually a new weapon, of slightly greater diameter, although it did employ three bolted sections, plus the 250-lb tail unit. The main sections were filled with Torpex and fused with three nose position pistol fuzes. The bomb required a team of four men to prepare and bolt together – a procedure which took two hours and fifteen minutes, and loading took a further 35 minutes. No 617 Sqn dropped most of the 186 to 193 weapons expended *(via Aeroplane)*

One of the legendary Bomber Command pilots, Wg Cdr Leonard Cheshire became CO of No 617 Sqn in the autumn of 1943, just as the unit began using the new SABS bombsight and 'big bombs'. Having completed four tours and over 100 missions, Cheshire was awarded the VC in September 1944 (*via Bruce Robertson*)

Lancaster B I ME554 of No 617 Sqn (seen here parked behind the YMCA Tea Car) participated in three of the *Tirpitz* missions, dropping *Tallboys* twice and 'Johnnie Walker' mines once. Assigned to the 'Dambuster' squadron in early 1944, where it was regularly flown by Sqn Ldr Tony Iveson and his crew, ME554 survived the war and was struck off charge on 15 January 1947 (*via Tony Iveson*)

Rested from operations while replacement crews were found, No 617 Sqn trained with a new gyro-stabilised bombsight – the Stabilised Automatic Bomb Sight (SABS) – which took account of the aircraft's speed, height, barometric pressure, wind speed and drift, and provided steering commands to the pilot. Bombing from heights of 20,000 ft, the squadron started to achieve average errors of less than 100 yards.

No 617 Sqn used the new sight and the 12,000-lb HC bomb to re-attack the Antheor Viaduct on 11/12 November, but were unable to collapse it, despite three very near misses. Under the command of another new CO, Wg Cdr Leonard Cheshire, No 617 Sqn attacked a number of V1 sites using its new bombs and bombsights on 16/17 and 30/31 December. On 8/9 February, the same weapon was used against the Gnome-Rhône engine plant at Limoges, demolishing the factory.

On 12 February, No 617 made another attempt against the Antheor Viaduct, but again failed to destroy the structure, although a number of attacks against French aircraft and explosives factories using the 12,000-lb HC bomb during March proved more successful, and a raid on the railway yards at Juvisy, near Paris, was spectacular. This target was marked by four new No 617 Sqn Mosquitos, and the 'Dambusters' Lancasters were followed by a full No 5 Group attack. A similar raid was flown against Munich the next night.

The 12,000-lb HC bomb was a primitive weapon, a crude three-section cylinder to which was attached a simple and rudimentary tail unit. It was thin-skinned, like the 4000- and 8000-lb bombs, and there was clearly a need for a more accurate heavy bomb which was easier to aim with greater precision, and which might also penetrate deeply before exploding, allowing it to 'shake' large structures to pieces like a small earthquake.

Dr Barnes Wallis of 'bouncing bomb' fame designed and developed two such weapons in parallel, the 12,000-lb *Tallboy* and the 22,000-lb *Grand Slam*. The bombs were fitted with a carefully designed tail unit which imparted a gentle spin as they fell, preventing them from toppling as they reached compressibility. This was routine, since both weapons could attain a terminal velocity of 2500 mph. The bombs were difficult

and expensive to manufacture (being cast and then machined from solid steel), and work on the ten-ton *Grand Slam* was slowed down to allow the smaller *Tallboy* to be rushed into service.

Tallboy was first used in anger on 9 June 1944 when No 617 Sqn dropped 25 devices on the French railway tunnel at Saumar. This had been constructed within a hill, and was previously thought to be virtually impregnable, but was also expected to be used by the Germans to send a Panzer division from southern France to reinforce the Normandy front (this unit had actually entrained on 8 June). The target was marked at one end by Wg Cdr Cheshire in a low-level Mosquito, and at the other by two more 'Mossies', before the target was illuminated by four No 83 Sqn Lancasters. The 19 *Tallboy* bombs were then dropped from 10,000 ft by No 617 Sqn, with six other aircraft carrying eight 1000-lb bombs and flares.

The *Tallboy* usually reached supersonic speed when dropped from altitude, and typically penetrated 100 ft before exploding. During the Saumar raid, several bombs left craters 70 ft deep and 100 ft wide, and one penetrated through to the tunnel, exploding and causing a major collapse, filling the tunnel with earth and rubble.

No 617 Sqn dropped 15 *Tallboys* on the E-boat pens at Le Havre on 14 June 1944. Three of the giant bombs penetrated the concrete roof and destroyed it, and the 206 conventional bombers which followed up (in two waves) destroyed every E-boat present. The daylight raid was escorted all the way by Fighter Command Spitfires, and only one Lancaster was lost. The next day No 617 Sqn attacked Boulogne with ten more *Tallboys*, part of a force which included 155 Lancasters and 130 Halifaxes. Another 133 boats were destroyed.

Once Germany started launching V1s from rapidly erectable prefabricated ramps, it became doubly necessary to destroy them while they were still in their storage sites, and before they could be deployed. These flying bombs were stockpiled in underground concrete shelters, which were perfect targets for *Tallboy*, and No 617 was tasked with attacking the suspected sites at Mimoyecques, Nucourt, Watten and Wizernes.

The squadron attacked Watten first, on 19 June 1944, with 19 aircraft dropping 15 *Tallboys*. Two missions against Wizernes on 20 and 22 June were aborted due to cloud cover, before the facility was destroyed by five *Tallboy* hits on 24 June 1944. The unit lost one Lancaster during the raid.

In the early war years, the German battleships *Bismarck* and *Tirpitz*, battlecruisers *Scharnhorst* and *Gneisenau* and pocket battleships *Graf Spee*, *Deutschland* (later *Lutzow*) and *Admiral von Scheer* had created

The 12,000-lb HC bomb could be carried by any Lancaster fitted with the bulged bomb-bay doors which had originally been fitted to allow aircraft to carry the smaller 8000-lb bomb – which was two 4,000-lb 'Cookies' simply joined together. These bulged bomb-bay doors are seen here on a B X, which later joined No 428 Sqn (and finished the war with No 419 Sqn). This Canadian-built aircraft also has the later Martin mid upper gun turret with twin 0.50 calibre Brownings, fitted further forward. KB783 returned to Canada post-war, where it became a ground instructional airframe *(via Phil Jarrett)*

55

havoc among Allied shipping. By 1944 only *Tirpitz*, the *Admiral von Scheer* and the *Admiral Hipper* remained.

Of these, *Tirpitz*, moored in a succession of Norwegian fjords, represented the greatest danger, poised as it was to attack the Arctic Convoys, or to sally forth into the North Atlantic. Bomber Command made a series of attempts to sink the ship, until mid-1944, when it was decided that the new *Tallboy* might represent the best weapon for the job.

The long distance between the UK and the Altenfjord ruled out a conventional 'out and return' op, and the decision was taken to fly the mission (Operation *Paravane*) from the USSR, with the attacking aircraft returning to their Soviet base before returning home. The force consisted of 20 SABS-equipped Lancasters from No 617 Sqn, 18 Lancasters from No IX Sqn fitted with conventional Mk XIV bombsights, a photographic Lancaster from No 463 Sqn, a PRU Mosquito and two Liberators carrying spares and groundcrew. Bad weather and incompatible radio beacons led to a number of the aircraft becoming lost en route to the USSR on 11 September. Six of these Lancasters were duly written off when they landed on marshy ground, and one returned to Britain.

Bad weather delayed the attack until 15 September, when 28 Lancasters set off, only to find an intense smoke screen masking the Altenfjord. 20 of the aircraft carried *Tallboys*, while six or seven were armed with giant 500-lb 'Johnny Walker' mines designed specifically for attacking capital ships in shallow water. Seventeen aircraft dropped *Tallboys*, while the other aircraft returned to Yagodnik with their *Tallboys* and 'Johnny Walkers' still aboard.

Unknown to the RAF, a solitary *Tallboy* did hit the ship's bow, however, causing major damage and causing *Tirpitz* to ship some 1500 tons of water, while other near misses caused further damage. The German Navy reluctantly concluded that the vessel's sea-going days were over, but it was decided to make minimal repairs and convert it into a floating coastal defence battery.

Tirpitz then slipped away, reappearing at Tromsö some 200 miles closer to Scotland, where it was to be repaired before being moored off the coast of Haaköy island. This made it possible to launch a second attack from Scotland, although the aircraft had to be fited with auxiliary fuel tanks taken from Wellingtons and Mosquitos. The installation of the latter made the aircraft two tons heavier than their normal weight limit, so they were stripped of their front turrets and other equipment, lightened, and fitted with more powerful Merlin 24 engines.

On 23/24 September No 617 Sqn led a No 5 Group attack on the Dort-mund-Ems Canal, which at last achieved a major breach after two direct hits with *Tallboys*, although 14 of the 136 attacking Lancasters were

Due to its internal carriage, there are relatively few photos of the 12,000-lb *Tallboy*. Here, one is being loaded aboard ED763/KC-Z of No 617 Sqn. Named *'HONOR'*, this aircraft was flown by Flt Lt Stuart Anning on the third of the attacks on the *Tirpitz* on 12 November 1944. The bomber also participated in a number of attacks against viaducts and other targets, dropping both 12,000-lb HC bombs and *Tallboys*. Initially issued to No 467 Sqn, ED763 saw all of its operational service with No 617 Sqn, and survived the war *(via Bruce Robertson)*

lost. No 617 Sqn returned to 'dambusting' on 7 October 1944, targeting the floodgates of the Kembs Dam at the Belfort Gap. The squadron attacked in two groups, a flight of six going in 'on the deck' and a second group of seven approaching at higher altitude (8000 ft). The German flak gunners initially concentrated on the high level aircraft, allowing one Lancaster to drop its bomb from low level, embedding the delay-fused *Tallboy*

in the floodgates. Two more Lancasters were shot down, but the first bomb then exploded, producing a huge torrent of water. Boats were swept away, some finally 'beaching' in nearby Switzerland.

Following this interlude, preparations were made for another attack against the *Tirpitz*. The Lancasters of Nos IX and 617 Sqn deployed forward to RAF Lossiemouth on 28 October, and at 0100 hrs on 29 October 20 from each squadron took off for Tromsö. When they arrived, they found the fjord covered by mist, and 32 *Tallboys* were dropped blind, all falling well wide. One aircraft was lost, forced-landing in Sweden.

Another attack was made on 12 November by 18 Lancasters from No 617 Sqn and 13 from No IX. *Tirpitz* was hit by at least three *Tallboys*, rolling over soon afterwards. The ship remained afloat, but upside down, and was a total loss.

CO Wg Cdr J B 'Willie' Tait, who had taken over No 617 Sqn from Cheshire in July 1944, was himself replaced in January 1945 by Gp Capt J E Fauquier, a distinguished pre-war Canadian bush pilot who had previously commanded the sole Canadian Pathfinder unit, No 405 Sqn, and who dropped a rank (from air commodore) to take the reigns of No 617.

Fauquier's first operation was an attack on U-boat pens at Bergen on 12 January 1945, leading 16 of his squadron's Lancasters, and 16 from No IX Sqn. The defences were alert, however, and two of the No 617 Sqn aircraft were lost, together with one from No IX. Three *Tallboys* penetrated the structure however, causing major damage. Two U-boats and a cargo ship were damaged, and a minesweeper was sunk. U-boat pens were attacked again on 3 February, when No 617 dropped *Tallboys* on facilities at Poortershaven, while No IX Sqn used them to attack Ijmuiden. No 617 made a return visit to Ijmuiden on 8 February.

Among the targets allocated to No 617 Sqn in early 1945 was the Bielefeld viaduct, which carried the main railway line between the Ruhr and Bremen and Hamburg. This

The German battleship *Tirpitz* fully capsized after the final attack by the Lancasters of Nos IX and 617 Sqns on 12 November 1944, during which it suffered several direct hits. The two units still dispute which one actually sank the ship, and a bulkhead removed from the wreck and kept as a trophy frequently changes hands as one squadron steals it from the other!
(via Bruce Robertson)

Tugs battle vainly to save the stricken *Tirpitz* after the 12 November attack by 31 Lancasters. The ship was hit by at least six 12,000-lb *Tallboys*, one of which caused an explosion in one of the vessel's magazines. Ironically, Hitler had already decreed that the ship should be decommissioned and used as a floating coastal defence battery after the first Lancaster raid on 15 September 1944, when the vessel had been hit in the bow by a single bomb *(via Bruce Robertson)*

PB592 was the first prototype B I (Special) *Grand Slam* carrier. The earlier 'dambusting' Lancaster was often referred to as the B I (Special), but should more properly be known as the Type 464 Provisioning Lancaster. The aircraft is seen here with a *Grand Slam* in place, the device having been painted black and white to allow for better interpretation of film of the test drop. The fins of the *Grand Slam* imparted spin to the bomb, which made it formidably accurate, following a very predictable (but very fast) trajectory *(via Phil Jarrett)*

Grand Slam trials began on 1 February 1945, and the first operational mission was flown on 13 March (although the aircraft was recalled after take off). The first live test drop was made at the Ashley Walk range in Hampshire, while the first combat use of the weapon was made against the Bielefeld Viaduct *(via Bruce Robertson)*

PB995 (also seen above) was the first aircraft in a production batch of 32 B I (Specials) built to carry the *Grand Slam*. Unlike later aircraft in the batch, this 'production prototype' (which never entered squadron service) retained all three of its gun turrets, and was used for trials by the A&AEE at Boscombe Down *(via Phil Jarrett)*

had been attacked on numerous occasions using small bombs, but remained unscathed. It seemed to be the perfect target for the *Tallboy*.

Nos IX and 617 Sqns attacked the viaduct three times during February (recalled on the 6th, attack abandoned on the 14th and on 22/23 February), dropping a total of 54 *Tallboys* with their customary precision, but with an equal lack of success. The marshy ground around the viaduct dramatically reduced the effectiveness of the 12,000-lb *Tallboy*, however,

and it became clear that the structure would need to be attacked using the *Tallboy's* big brother, the 22,000-lb *Grand Slam*.

The bomb had been developed in parallel with the *Tallboy*, which had been rushed into service for the post D-Day interdiction campaign. By early 1945, however, the bigger weapon was also ready for use, along with a batch of aircraft modified to carry the weapon. The 32 Lancaster B I (Special) aircraft built to carry the 22,000-lb *Grand Slam* had more powerful Merlin engines, a strengthened undercarriage and a cut-away bomb-bay with a chain-like bomb restraint/release mechanism.

Prototype PB592 had begun flight trials on 1 February 1945, along with PB995, the first production *Grand Slam* aircraft. Two B Is (PD112 and PB996) were delivered to No 617 Sqn on 13 March – the same day that the trials aircraft made their first live drop on the Ashley Walk range in Hampshire.

The intention had been to send out two *Grand Slam*-carrying Lancasters against the Bielefeld and Arnsberg Viaducts that afternoon, but in the event one was unserviceable, so the other set off with a gaggle of aircraft carrying *Tallboy*. These encountered bad weather and only one aircraft bombed at Arnsberg, with two attacking alternate targets. The planned raid was repeated the following day, with 32 Lancasters and five Mosquitos. This time Nos IX and 617 Sqn met with success, the single *Grand Slam* penetrating far below the surface before exploding. Two of the Viaduct's pylons and spans collapsed into the resulting crater, while several more adjacent spans, weakened by the *Grand Slam*, were destroyed by the *Tallboys* dropped by 14 of the accompanying Lancasters, leaving a 100-yard gap.

The Bielefeld Viaduct after being attacked by No 617 Sqn, which dropped one *Grand Slam* and several *Tallboys* on the structure on 14 March 1945. The large craters visible in this picture are those left by the *Tallboys*, while the *Grand Slam* made a rather smaller hole (next to the standing pillar in the gap in the Viaduct), penetrating deep and exploding underground *(via Bruce Robertson)*

A *Grand Slam* bomb drops away from one of No 617 Sqn's Lancaster B I Specials. Early *Grand Slam* aircraft were delivered in standard Bomber Command night camouflage, but later machines wore day bomber colours, with a low demarcation line and light grey undersides. PB996/YZ-C was the first operational aircraft from the production batch, although No 617 Sqn had already received PD112/YZ-S. PB996 participated in at least five *Grand Slam* attacks during March 1945, and was eventually struck off charge on 19 November 1947 *(via Francis K Mason)*

The next *Grand Slam* target was the Arnsberg Viaduct, which carried the main railway line from the Ruhr to Kassel, and was located midway between the Möhne and Sorpe Dams. An abortive raid was mounted on 15 March, but conditions were poor and one of the two No 617 Sqn *Grand Slam* aircraft brought its weapon home, along with several of the 15 No IX Sqn *Tallboy*-armed Lancasters. No fewer than five *Grand Slams* were finally dropped on the Arnsberg Viaduct on 19 March, along with thirteen *Tallboys*. All of the bombs fell within a 200-yard circle, blowing a 50-yard gap in the viaduct, and severely damaging the structure that remained standing.

No 617 Sqn attacked the Nienburg bridge between Bremen and Hannover on 22 March. A *Grand Slam* and a *Tallboy* exploded at each end of the central span, lifting it into the air, where it was hit by another *Tallboy*. The squadron brought five unused *Grand Slams* and eleven *Tallboys* home to Woodhall Spa. The unit made its last *Grand Slam* bridge attack on 23 March, bombing a railway bridge at Bremen and scoring direct hits with two *Grand Slams* and two *Tallboys*.

On 27 March 18 No 617 Sqn Lancasters (12 armed with *Grand Slam* and six with *Tallboy*) led 100 Main Force bombers to the U-boat pens at Farge, at the mouth of the Weser. Two *Grand Slams* brought down much of the roof, and the other bombs rendered the remaining structure unsafe.

Two abortive attempts were made to bomb the remaining pocket battleship *Lutzow* at Swinemünde on 13 and 15 April, before a successful mission was flown on 16 April 1945. A near-miss tore open the ship's hull and it sank in shallow water, partly submerged. One aircraft was lost, and all but two of the 18 bombers were damaged by the intense flak.

No 617 Sqn participated in the attack on Berchtesgaden on 25 April and dropped 16 *Tallboys* on the SS barracks, its final attack of the war.

Post-war trials of *Grand Slams* against redundant U-boat pens were undertaken by No XV Sqn during Operation *Front Line* in 1946. PD131 had previously served with No 617 Sqn (with whom it had bombed Berchtesgaden) as YZ-A, before becoming LS-V with No XV. It was struck off charge on 19 May 1947 *(via Phil Jarrett)*

BACK TO GERMANY

Control of the Bomber Command heavy bombers reverted to the Air Staff on 14 September 1944, although it was almost immediately committed to further tactical operations, supporting the airborne operation *Market-Garden*. Lancasters bombed airfields at Hopsten, Leeuwarden, Steenwijk and Rheine and flak positions in both Moerijk, on 16/17 September, and near Flushing the next day. Tactical operations also continued in France, where Boulogne was attacked by 370 Lancasters and 351 Halifaxes on 17 September, in preparation for a push by ground troops. The garrison surrendered soon afterwards. The Command then turned its weight on Calais, attacking on 20, 24, 25, 26, 27 and 28 September.

This was perhaps a blessing, since arguments still raged as to the strategy which the Bomber Command squadrons should follow. 'Bomber' Harris was still expected to attack the German garrisons in the Channel ports and around Antwerp while the Allies fought to gain more convenient continental port facilities than Brest. Bomber Command also continued to give some direct support to the Allied armies, but these tasks required relatively little effort.

Some, including Harris himself, favoured a return to the general bombing of German cities in an effort to deflate the morale of the German industrial work force. Harris continued to believe that this would cause a complete collapse, saving the Allied armies the losses which would accompany the storming of the rest of the Reich.

But Harris's was a minority view. Sir Charles Portal and most of the Air Ministry preferred to concentrate on the German oil and synthetic oil industry, which, they felt, would rob the Wehrmacht of its mobility and would effectively ground the Luftwaffe. Eisenhower's air commander (and second in command), Air Chief Marshal Sir Arthur Tedder, favoured continued interdiction of German communications and transport facilities, impressed by Bomber Command's extraordinary contribution to the victory in Normandy.

Harris viewed both of these as being 'panacea targets' and when ordered, on 1 November 1944, to 'maintain and if possible intensify' pressure on the 'enemy petroleum industry and oil supplies', his private response was to scribble 'Here we go round the Mulberry bush!' in the margin.

Harris was forced to pay lip-service to this directive, and to directives to attack the transport system, but did so unwillingly, finding every possible excuse (usually weather related) to continue with his own strategy, and camouflaging area attacks on cities by nominally aiming at oil or transport targets within them.

The task facing Bomber Command became progressively easier, and its losses plummeted. One year after the Battle of Berlin, in October 1944, Bomber Command's loss rate had fallen to less than one per cent. During the last six months of the war, Bomber Command lost only 649 'heavies' – representing significantly less than one per cent of the total despatched. This was an obvious morale booster, since it meant that statistically, two out of three bomber crews could expect to complete a 30-mission tour of operations. Occasional raids would still meet fierce opposition and suffer correspondingly heavy losses, although there were an increasing number of missions that were effectively 'milk runs'.

When Bomber Command returned to Harris's direct control, it was a very much more capable and effective force than it had been, with a larger proportion of Lancasters, the Stirlings and Merlin-engined Halifaxes having been withdrawn from the Main Force. Bomber Command had 51 Lancaster squadrons by the end of 1944, and 57 by VE-Day. Those Halifaxes which remained in Nos 4 and 6 Groups (the latter already re-equipping with Lancasters) were all radial-engined Mk IIIs, and, increasingly, the much improved Mk VIs.

No 3 Group, whose aircraft were now almost fully equipped with G-H blind-bombing radar equipment, was usually able to operate autonomously, like No 5 Group, leaving Nos 1, 4, 6 and 8 Groups as the 'Main Force', except when a maximum effort was required.

With the perimeter of the Reich contracting, and a rapidly reducing list of potential targets (many falling into Allied hands, others having been 'bombed to capacity'), many expected the intensity of Bomber Command operations to slow down. In fact, the Command dropped almost as great a tonnage of bombs during the last nine months of the war as it had done during the whole of the rest of the conflict, with this period accounting for a staggering 46 per cent of ordnance expended.

The final months of the conflict also saw Bomber Command mount some of its largest and heaviest attacks, with raids involving more than 700 Lancasters. The Command destroyed a number of cities which had previously defied its efforts, and attacked a number of smaller, less industrialised towns. This strategy would bring great criticism post-war, when the apparently unnecessary destruction of cultural landmarks and medieval town centres was noted.

This otherwise anonymous No 50 Sqn Lancaster wears the name of Phyllis Dixey, star of the Whitehall Theatre and the first stripper to perform in the West End. Miss Dixey was a 'Forces Favourite', who travelled widely to entertain the troops. While she certainly regularly played at Aldershot's Theatre Royal, it is not known whether this 'ladylike stripper' visited any theatres close to No 50 Sqn's Skellingthorpe base (*via Phil Jarrett*)

As the Allies advanced through Europe, Germany lost many of its early warning sites, while the RAF was able to use navigation beacons which were on European soil, extending the range of systems like *Gee*, G-H and *Oboe*. The bombers themselves remained at their bases in eastern England though, complicating the task of German counter-action (by night intruders, for example) and obviating the need to repair and upgrade captured airfields closer to the ever-shrinking perimeter of the Reich. Few airfields in France would have been capable of hosting a unit of fully laden 'heavies', and the few exceptions had generally been badly bombed.

Even before D-Day, the long range escort fighters which facilitated the USAAF's daylight bombing campaign had begun to achieve air superiority over Europe by day, and were responsible for the destruction of significant numbers of twin-engined fighters which might otherwise have been pressed into use against Bomber Command by night. Following the invasion, more German aircraft and aircrew were thrown into ground attack missions, while longer-ranging Allied fighter-bombers made life increasingly difficult at German nightfighter airfields. The Mosquito nightfighters were also extremely active, taking a steady toll of the defenders.

The surviving German nightfighter crews found themselves operating in a much more difficult environment during the closing phases of the war. Quite apart from the danger posed by Allied fighters, No 100 Group was increasingly effective in jamming the nightfighters' SN-2 airborne radar, using *Piperack*, while *Jostle* jammed the entire Luftwaffe VHF radio band. German-speaking operators in Britain broadcast confusing and contradictory instructions to nightfighter crews using *Corona*, while German attempts to at least give an indication of the likely target to night-fighter crews by broadcasting different kinds of music (jazz meant Berlin, a waltz meant Munich, etc) were stymied when the British blanketed the airwaves with the Old Comrades march – the German musical code which indicated that the bombers had departed!

On top of all this, the RAF's 'heavies' were becoming better able to defend themselves, with improved armament. AGLT (Automatic Gun Laying Turret) or *Village Inn* gave the Lancaster a rearward facing radar

The Lancaster had poor ditching characteristics (except in radial-engined B II form), and this gently floating airframe is something of an exception. Bent propeller blades indicate that all four props were turning when the aircraft hit the water *(via Phil Jarrett)*

which could be used to automatically 'lay' the guns in the modified Frazer Nash FN 121 turret, and was trialled by No 1323 Flt at Warboys and by Nos 514 and 460 Sqns, the latter unit flying operationally with the device in July 1944. Plans to fit Hispano 20 mm cannon in the mid-upper turret of the Lancaster were frustrated by centre of gravity considerations (and by delays to the Bristol B 17 turret), and the B VII, with 0.50-in guns in a new Martin turret located further forward, was too late to see active service.

A new tail turret was installed on some aircraft, however. Messrs Rose Brothers of Gainsborough designed a new tail turret with two 0.50-in guns and a more open, 'high visibility' design, and this was deployed on No 150 Sqn aircraft from October 1944, subsequently becoming standard on about 180 Lancasters. The 0.50-in guns offered a considerable increase in range and hitting power, and the

new turret could be retrofitted in place of a standard FN 20 turret in only three-and-a-half hours.

As if this were not enough, the Luftwaffe was also running out of fuel. Production and imports had once totalled one million tonnes per month, but in the wake of D-Day this slumped to only 300,000 tonnes. Often, there was insufficient fuel to respond to attacks. Britain's Joint Intelligence Committee dryly noted 'an increasing paralysis of the German War Machine'.

The standard Lancaster tail armament consisted of an impressive looking quartet of 0.303-in machine guns mounted in a Frazer Nash FN 20 turret, although these weapons lacked the reach and punch to be of much more than nuisance value to a determined multi-gunned Bf 110, Ju 88, He 219, Fw 190, Bf 109 or Me 262 pilot *(via Phil Jarrett)*

Above and left
The Rose turret mounted a pair of 0.50-in Browning machine guns, which had much greater 'stopping power' and range than the puny rifle-calibre 0.303s. The turret also offered the gunner a far better all-round view, and, in an emergency, allowed egress through the back of the turret, making escape much easier *(via Francis K Mason)*

Photographs of frontline aircraft fitted with the Rose turret are relatively rare, this particular B III (LM732/TC-C) serving with No 170 Sqn at Dunholm Lodge and Hemswell between September 1944 and April 1945. It had initially been delivered to No 625 Sqn on 9 September 1944, and flew one raid (to Frankfurt) with the unit prior to transferring to No 170 Sqn. LM732 was struck off charge on 25 August 1947 *(via Francis K Mason)*

No 106 Sqn flight engineer Sgt Norman Cyril Jackson won a VC following a raid on Schweinfurt on 26 April 1944, having literally crawled out onto the wing of his Lancaster (ME669) to extinguish a raging fire, using his parachute as a lifeline. With the bomber flying at over 200 mph, he was quickly blown off through the conflagration (which also set his parachute alight), but survived the subsequent descent, albeit with severely burned hands and a broken ankle. Jackson's Lancaster crashed, although four other crewmembers successfully bailed out prior to its eventual demise *(via Bruce Robertson)*

Despite the clear success of the campaign against the German oil industry, Harris burned to return his Lancasters to pure area attacks against enemy cities, and while claiming to be targeting oil facilities whenever conditions permitted, loudly disagreed with the policy. This prompted a series of letters between Harris and the Chief of the Air Staff, Sir Charles Portal, who urged his subordinate to 'Put all possible effort into eliminating major enemy oil plants. I believe that the task is within the capability of the strategic bomber forces if they put their hearts into it. If they do, Strategic Bombing will go down to history as a deciding factor in winning this war'. Harris finally threatened to resign, and was given his head to fight the bomber war as he saw fit.

Attacks against German cities had not entirely stopped before 14 September, with large scale attacks against Aachen (11/12 April and 24/25 and 27/28 May), Bremen (18/19 August), Brunswick (22/23 May and 12/13 August), Darmstadt (25/26 August and 11/12 September), Dortmund (22/23 May), Duisberg (21/22 May), Düsseldorf (22/23 April), Emden (6 September), Essen (26/27 April), Frankfurt (12/13 September), Friedrichshafen (27/28 April), Gelsenkirchen (12/13 June and 13 September), Hamburg (28/29 July), Homberg (20/21 July and 27 August), Karlsrühe (24/25 April), Kiel (23/24 July and 26/27 August), Köln (20/21 April), Königsberg (26/27 and 29/30 August), Mönchengladbach (9/10 September), Munich

65

This is the aftermath of a Lancaster raid on Frankfurt on 12/13 September 1944. This raid was destined to be the city's last major attack of the war *(via Phil Jarrett)*

(24/25 April), Münster (12 September), Osnabrück (13 September), Russelsheim (12/13 and 25/26 August), Schweinfurt (26/27 April), Stettin (16/17 and 29/30 August), Stuttgart (24/25, 25/26 and 28/29 July) and Wesseling (21/22 June and 18/19 July).

The attack on Brunswick on 12/13 August was an experimental mission made without Pathfinder support and relying entirely on H_2S carried by Main Force aircraft. The 27 August 1944 attack on Homberg marked Bomber Command's first major daylight raid on Germany since August 1941, and was escorted by nine Spitfire squadrons outbound and by seven squadrons on the withdrawal. No bombers were lost. Some of these attacks were extremely heavy, with the attack on Darmstadt on 11/12 September killing a reported 8433 people (and possibly as many as 12,000), and effectively destroying the city in one devastating firestorm.

The night before they were officially transferred back to the control of the Air Ministry, the Bomber Command 'heavies' hit Frankfurt (where many local fireman were missing, tackling the blaze at Darmstadt, and where fires burned until the evening of 15 September) and 'erased' the northern and western parts of Stuttgart's centre. Bomber Command lost 17 of 378 Lancasters on the Frankfurt raid, and four of the 204 despatched against Stuttgart.

Bomber Command attacked a variety of targets between these attacks and Operation *Thunderclap* – the historic and infamous attack on Dresden. These included straightforward area attacks and raids on oil-related and transport targets. The bald name Köln, for example, usually covered attacks on railway yards, while attacks described as being targeted against Politz and Dortmund were usually aimed at nearby oil plants.

Although control of the 'heavies' passed back to Bomber Command on 14 September 1944, the Lancasters remained committed to tactical duties. This aircraft from No 576 Sqn (PD235/UL-N²) was lost on 24 September during an attack on Calais *(via Bruce Robertson)*

A list of targets of major Lancaster raids during the winter of 1944-45 included the U-boat pens at Bergen (attacked on 4 and 28/29 October and 12 January 1945). Other targets included Bingen (22/23 December), Bochum (4/5 November), Bonn (18 October, 21/22 and 28/29 December and 4/5 February), Bottrop (30 November and 3/4 February), Bremen (6/7 October), Bremerhaven (18/19 September), Brunswick (14/15 October), Castrop-Rauxel (11 and 21/22 November), Dortmund (6/7 October, 11/12, 15 and 29 November, 3 December, 1/2 and 3 January and 3/4 February), Dortmund-Ems canal (4/5, 6/7 and 21/22 November, 1 January and 7/8 February), Duisberg (14-15 October, 30 November/1 December, 8 and 17/18 December and 22/23 January), Düsseldorf (2/3 November), Emmerich (7 October), Essen (23/24 and 25 October, 28/29 November and 12/13 December), Fulda (26 November), Freiburg (27/28 November), Gelsenkirchen (6 and 23 November, 22/23 January and 4/5 February), Giessen (6/7 December), Gdynia (18/19 December), Hagen (2/3 December), Hamm (5 December), Hanau (6/7 January), Hannover (5/6 January), Harburg (11/12 November), Heilbronn (4/5 December), Homberg (25 October and 2, 8 and 20 November), Houffalize (30/31 December), Kaiserslautern (27/28 September), Karlsrühe (26/27 September, 4/5 December and 2/3 February), Kiel (15/16 September), Kleve (7 October), Koblenz (6/7, 20/21 and 21 November and 22/23 and 29 December), Köln (28, 30/31 and 31 October/1 November, 27 November, 21/22, 23, 24/25, 28 and 30/31 December and 28 January), Krefeld (11 and 29 January and 8/9 February), Leipzig/Leuna (6/7 December and 14/15 January), Leverkeusen (26 October), Ludwigshafen (15/16 December, 2/3 and 5 January and 1/2 February), Magdeburg (16/17 January), Mainz (1/2 February), Mönchengladbach (19/20 September, 28/29 December and 1 February), Munich (26/27 November, 17/18 December and 7/8 January), Münster (18 November), Neuss (23/24 September, 22 October, 27/28 and 28/29 November and 6/7 January), Nuremberg (2/3 January), Oberhausen (4 December), Opladen (27/28 December), Osnabrück (6/7 December), Osterfeld (11 and 31 December/1 January and 4/5 February), Pölitz (21/22 December, 13/14 January and 8/9 February),

River Scheldt gun batteries (11 and 12 October), Saarbrücken (5/6 October, 13, 13/14 and 14 January), Scholven (29/30 December), Siegen (1/2 February), Soest (5/6 December), Solingen (4/5 November), Stuttgart (19/20 October and 28/29 January), Trier (19, 21 and 23 December), Troisdorf (29/30 December), Trondheim (22/23 November), Ulm (17/18 December), Vohwinkel (31 December and 1/2 January), Walcheren (3, 7, 11 and 17 October), Wanne-Eickel (12 October, 9 and 18/19 November, 16/17 January and 2/3 and 8/9 February), Wiesbaden (2/3 February), Wilhelmshaven (14 September, 5, 15/16, 21, 28, 29 and 30 October) and Witten (12 December).

Of these, the attack on Mönchengladbach on 19/20 September cost the life of the Master Bomber Wg Cdr Guy Gibson of 'Dambuster' fame. Flying a Mosquito that evening, Gibson and his navigator crashed after the raid, perhaps due either to engine trouble or flak.

The raid against Neuss on 23/24 September marked the last operation by the B II, two No 514 Sqn aircraft participating. Ironically, with the improved tactical situation over Germany, the need for the Lancaster to fly at its maximum height had disappeared, and the B II, with its less vulnerable air-cooled radial engines and improved performance at slightly lower altitudes, was in many respects a better aircraft for the job.

Whereas most successful wartime aircraft were produced in a succession of improved variants, the three versions of the Lancaster which saw extensive service were the same basic type, differing only in place of manufacture or engine supply. Thus the B III was essentially a B I with Packard-built engines, and the B X was its Canadian-built equivalent.

This Lancaster B VI (JB675) flew with Nos 7 and 405 Sqns before joining No 635 for a single operation. It then returned to No 7 Sqn, followed by No 76 Sqn, before returning to the RAE. It is seen here during early trials at Boscombe Down in January 1944 *(via Phil Jarrett)*

Lancaster B VI ND673/F2-V was photographed 'out to grass' at Farnborough post-war, albeit still in full No 635 Sqn markings – including the unit's G-H Master Bomber tail fin stripes. This is believed to be the only photo of a No 635 Sqn B VI *(via Bruce Robertson)*

Avro had, of course, considered a number of improved and advanced Lancaster versions, including impressive-looking pressurised 'stratospheric bombers'. The Lancaster B IV and B V were improved versions intended to replace the B I, III and X, and to operate over longer ranges. These became the Lincoln B I and B II, which were too late to see wartime service.

As an interim, the Lincoln's Merlin 85/87 engine was fitted to a handful of B IIIs to produce the interim (but still significantly improved) Lancaster B VI. Two prototype conversions were followed by seven 'production' conversions, but by this time maintaining commonality on the Lancaster squadrons was felt to be more important than improved performance, and no further conversions were undertaken and there was no production of the B VI. Five of the seven aircraft did see brief operational service with No 635 Sqn, three of them after use by No 7 Sqn. Nos 83, 405 and 582 Sqns also briefly used the type.

The attack on Dortmund on 6/7 October represented the biggest effort by No 6 (RCAF) Group of the war, with 45 Lancasters and 248 Halifaxes. The raid opened what came to be known as the second battle of the Ruhr, which included Operation *Hurricane*.

The Allies launched Operation *Hurricane* on 14 October, under which the USAAF and Bomber Command attacked targets 'around the clock'. The Directive launching the operation dictated that 'In order to demonstrate to the enemy the overwhelming superiority of the Allied Air Forces in this theatre, the intention is to apply within the shortest practical period the maximum effort of the Royal Air Force Bomber Command

An unidentified crew pose with their No 7 Sqn Lancaster at Oakington, in Cambridgeshire, during early 1945. Interestingly, only two of the seven-man crew are NCOs
(via Bruce Robertson)

and the VIII US Bomber Command against objectives in the densely populated Ruhr'.

Some 519 Lancasters, 474 Halifaxes and 20 Mosquitos dropped 3574 tons of HE and 820 tons of incendiaries on Duisberg, with 13 Lancasters and one Halifax falling victim to enemy flak. The USAAF despatched 1251 further bombers that day, before Bomber Command sent out another 498 Lancasters and 468 Halifaxes (with 39 Mosquitos) in two waves that night (14/15

October), dropping another 4040 tons of HE and 500 tons of incendiaries. Sometimes Bomber Command crews would fly to the same target by day and then by night, snatching a few hours sleep between the missions, as happened during the maximum effort against Duisberg. On the same night, No 5 Group sortied 233 Lancasters against Brunswick.

When No 3 Group attacked Bonn on 18 October it was the first fully independent operation by the group, commanded by Air Vice Marshal R Harrison. The idea was that the group would use G-H to find its targets when the ground was obscured by cloud, and when cloud tops did not exceed 18,000 ft. About a third of No 3 Group's Lancasters were equipped with G-H, and these wore prominent coloured fins. Non G-H-equipped aircraft were expected to find and formate on a G-H aircraft in the target area and bomb when the G-H aircraft did. Bonn (previously unbombed) was targeted so that post-strike reconnaissance would give an accurate impression of the damage caused by No 3 Group's G-H aircraft. These proved devastatingly effective, tearing the heart out of the old city and burning its most historic buildings and university.

On 16 November 1944 Bomber Command briefly returned to a more tactical role. In the area between Aachen and the Rhine, the US First and Ninth Armies were about to attack, and Bomber Command was tasked

Sir Allan Burns, Governor of the Gold Coast, and his wife Lady Burns are seen during a visit to No 218 'Gold Coast' Sqn in August 1945, with Methwold Station Commander Gp Capt Brotherhood, OC No 218 Sqn Wg Cdr W J Smith, and Air Commodore J Silvester from No 3 Group. The aircraft in the background wears its full wartime colours, including G-H Master Bomber bars on the tailfins *(via Bruce Robertson)*

Even by late 1944 many Lancasters still lacked H_2S and other aids, as shown by No 550 Sqn B I LL796 at North Killingholme, on Humberside. The plain red codes worn by aircraft outside No 5 Group are also evident. Having previously served with No 576 Sqn, this aircraft went missing on the 12/13 July 1944 mission to Stuttgart *(via Francis K Mason)*

with attacking three towns just behind the lines. It despatched 1188 aircraft in total, with 485 Lancasters bombing Düren, 78 bombing Jülich (along with 413 Halifaxes) and 182 No 3 Group aircraft attacking Heinsberg. The three towns were destroyed, Düren suffering 3127 fatalities, but the US advance was bogged down and proved costly.

When Bomber Command attacked Duisberg on 30 November complete cloud cover dictated a 'Wanganui' attack. This saw *Oboe* Mosquitos drop red target markers, on which No 635 Sqn's Wg Cdr Dennis Witt dropped his green flares accurately enough to ensure that bombing was effective and fairly concentrated. Duisberg lost 528 more houses and 246 of its people in the attack. This was Witt's 100th heavy bomber mission, and it proved to be his last, since PFF chief Don Bennett screened him from further operations and recommended him for a well-deserved DSO.

Bomber Command mounted 15 major daylight attacks against German towns during November, losing 39 aircraft in 3233 sorties. That same month No 150 Sqn joined No 1 Group at Hemswell, further swelling Bomber Command's Lancaster force.

A sharp deterioration in the weather (with a commensurate difficulty in obtaining good reconnaissance photography) led to a reduction in daylight attacks during December, although some missions were flown after the German army launched its offensive in the Ardennes on 16 December. Much attention was focused against German airfields, specifically those in Köln (through which most German reinforcements were expected to pass), St Vith (attacked on 26 December) and Houffalize (30/31 December). No 6 Group gained another Lancaster unit during December in the shape of No 434 Sqn at Croft.

December also saw the first attack made against an oil target in eastern Germany. Leuna (targeted on 6/7 December) was 250 miles from Germany's western border, and fully 500 miles from Bomber Command's East Anglian bases.

These final missions of 1944 saw many examples of quiet heroism, the majority of which went unremarked, as usual. But on 23 December 1944, 110-mission veteran Sqn Ldr Robert Anthony Maurice Palmer DFC of No 109 Sqn forsook his Mosquito for a G-H-equipped No 582 Sqn

This dramatic photograph was taken during the daylight raid on Rheydt's railway marshalling yards on 27 December 1944. A solitary Lancaster (out of a force of 200 that were sortied) and a Mosquito (of 11 despatched) were lost during the mission. The concentration of bombs around the target (shown dotted) is noteworthy *(via Francis K Mason)*

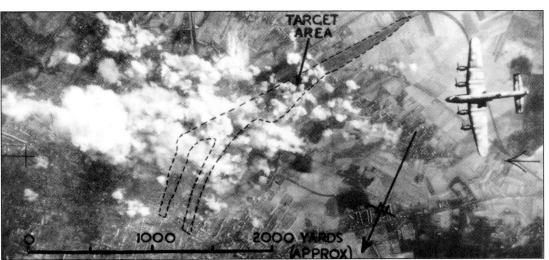

Sqn Ldr Anthony Maurice Palmer of No 582 Sqn was lost during a daylight attack against Köln's marshalling yards on 23 December 1944. A veteran of the first Thousand Bomber raid against the same city in 1942, Palmer's outstanding career was marked with the award of a posthumous VC (via Bruce Robertson)

Flt Sgt George Thompson, a wireless operator with No IX Sqn, won a posthumous VC after going to the aid of the rear and mid-upper gunners in his burning Lancaster during a raid on the Dortmund-Ems canal on 1 January 1945. He died of his wounds three weeks later, but saved the life of one of his comrades (via Bruce Robertson)

Lancaster, in which he led 27 Lancasters in an attack against Köln's marshalling yards. Palmer's aircraft was badly hit by flak during the run in to the target, and two engines and the cockpit were set ablaze, but he maintained his heading and dropped his bombs on target – the rest of the formation dropping on his signal as was routine during G-H attacks. His aircraft then spun in, killing all aboard, but winning the courageous pilot a posthumous VC.

Half of the attacking formation was lost, but the raid destroyed much of the material being massed to support von Runstedt's Ardennes offensive. Capt Edwin Swales of No 582 Sqn (who would later win a VC) was awarded the DFC for his part in this Köln railway yards raid.

1945 opened with another VC-winning act of heroism by a Lancaster crewman. During an attack against the Dortmund-Ems canal, wireless operator Flt Sgt George Thompson of No IX Sqn went to the aid of his mid-upper gunner, unconscious in a burning turret, dragging him clear despite the fire and exploding ammunition. Having beaten out the flames, suffering severe burns in the process, Thompson then rescued the tail gunner, braving the flames again. Suffering frostbite when he fought his way back to the cockpit to report to the captain, Thompson was so badly injured that the pilot initially failed to recognise him. The WO then looked after his comrades until the aircraft made a successful crash landing. He died of his injuries three weeks later.

While German efforts to counter the US daylight raids became more desperate during January, with several documented instances of deliberate rammings by fighter pilots, the Luftwaffe's nightfighter arm continued to rely on professionalism and skill, despite losses (to British action and postings to other branches of the force) and fuel shortages. On 7/8 February, for example, during an attack on Ladbergen on the Dortmund–Ems canal, five Lancasters and a single Halifax were downed by the *Schräge Musik* cannon wielded by Hauptmann Gerhard Raht, the *Gruppenkommandeur* of I./NJG 2, in his Ju 88. A Knight's Cross winner, Raht survived the war with 58 night kills from 171 missions.

On 2/3 January Bomber Command finally took its revenge on the city of Nuremberg, 514 Lancasters and seven Mosquitos destroying the castle, the Rathaus, most of the city's churches and some 2000 medieval houses and 4640 more modern flats and houses. 1838 people were killed, and the MAN and Siemens factories were severely damaged. Four Lancasters were lost, and two more crashed in France.

When 347 Lancasters attacked Royan on 4/5 January they killed large numbers of French civilians. The town was being held by a particularly stubborn German garrison, which prevented Allied use of the port of Bordeaux. Besieged by Resistance forces (officered by Gen de Gaulle's Free French regulars), the town held out, and when it was suggested that only Germans and collaborators remained there, it was decided to bomb Royan into submission. Unfortunately, the suggestion was erroneous, although it was soon acknowledged that Bomber Command was blameless, having received poor intelligence from Supreme Headquarters Allied Expeditionary Force (SHAEF).

Bomber Command again returned briefly to tactical operations on 7/8 February 1945, sending 156 Lancasters and 292 Halifaxes against the town of Goch and 295 Lancasters against Kleve. The bombers attacked from below cloud, helping to clear the way for an attack by the British XXX Corps, led by the 15th (Scottish) Division. The raid was stopped when thick smoke obscured the target, but caused enough damage to block the British advance through Kleve!

A No 467 Sqn Lancaster is seen being serviced at its dispersal at Waddington, in Lincolnshire, in the spring of 1945. The large code letter repeated on the tailfin was unusual, and very much a late-war addition to the colour scheme on those aircraft marked with it *(via Bruce Robertson)*

Even after the destruction of the most important targets and cities, Bomber Command's attacks continued unabated. There was an understandable desire to do everything possible to erode the defences which stood in the way of the Allied advance, and thereby to 'get it over with' as quickly as possible. The German counter attack in the Ardennes (the so-called Battle of the Bulge) had proved a costly defeat for Hitler, but had demonstrated that the Wehrmacht was far from beaten, thereby justifying ever greater efforts to achieve victory. It had also set back Allied plans for a crossing of the Rhine, delaying the final assault on Germany.

The Allied powers still wanted to 'teach Germany a lesson', desiring to impose cost and punishment on an enemy which had been a thorn in their sides for decades. It is easy to forget that in 1945 European nations had either been at war with Germany, or threatened by the spectre of war with Germany, for most of the century.

Bomber Command thus gained new targets, including a number of smaller cities and larger towns which had not been attacked before 1944. These were often communications hubs, whose destruction was intended to complicate the Wehrmacht's task in deploying reinforcements to the front by causing a massive refugee problem, as well as by destroying key parts of Germany's transport infrastructure. They were often little more than country towns which had the misfortune to stradle a vital crossroads or a large road or railway. Few boasted any important military targets.

Bomber Command's Lancaster force continued to expand, as No 6 Group converted from the Halifax. During January, the two units at Skipton-on-Swale – Nos 424 and 433 Sqns – converted.

Some senior Allied politicians already feared that the USSR would be the 'next problem' for the Western Allies, and hoped to limit the extent of the Soviet push into Poland, Czechoslovakia and Germany. Churchill, by

Lancaster B I *PRINCESS PAT* (NG347/QB-P) of No 424 Sqn is seen here with no guns in its front turret, presumably during a training sortie. The aircraft wears a Vargas-style pin-up on its nose – a popular adornment on No 424 Sqn's later Lancasters. This aircraft served exclusively with the Canadian squadron *(via Phil Jarrett)*

contrast, was still keen to do what he could to assist Stalin, and insisted that Bomber Command extend its operations to eastern cities which lay in the path of the Red Army advance, or through which German reinforcements might flow to the Eastern Front. Churchill had long been urged to bomb the German population by Stalin, who believed that it was the only useful second front which the Allies could open, and that it represented the only way of breaking German morale. Stalin approved the new strategy of concentrating on East German targets at the Yalta Conference, and Bomber Command gained a raft of new targets in the eastern part of Germany.

The most obvious of these was Dresden, whose destruction has (rightly or wrongly) sullied and tarnished the reputation of Bomber Command, and which has even been cited by some as an example of an Allied 'War Crime'. Harris has personally shouldered much of the 'blame' for Dresden, although Churchill himself had urged 'absolutely devastating, exterminating attack by very heavy bombers upon the Nazi homeland' since July 1940, and had been enthusiastically supported by Portal, the Chief of the Air Staff. Under Operation *Thunderclap*, Bomber Command was told to make heavy attacks on Dresden, Chemnitz and Leipzig.

For most of the war the bomber campaign had fallen far short of this kind of absolute storm of terror and destruction. Night after night tens of precious bombers and their irreplaceable crews had failed to return from missions which managed to damage a house or two and kill the odd cow, as bombs were almost randomly scattered within a huge area usually (but by no means always) somewhere vaguely near the intended target. Depressingly often, Bomber Command casualties far outnumbered German casualties on the ground. It was Dresden's misfortune to be targeted at a time when Bomber Command's accuracy had reached new levels, and the destructiveness of its weapons was at its peak, while the defences were relatively powerless.

The operation was expected to begin with a raid on Dresden by USAAF day bombers, but bad weather prevented this, and the first attack was made at night by the RAF. On 13/14 February some 796 Lancasters and nine Mosquitos attacked Dresden in two waves. The 244 Lancasters sent by No 5 Group attacked first, dropping their 800 tons of bombs with modest success, while the second wave (with full Pathfinder support) proved more accurate, and their 1800 tons of bombs created an immense firestorm, killing more than 50,000 people. The Bomber Command attack was followed by daylight raids by USAAF B-17s and B-24s on 14 and 15 February, a further 700 tons of American bombs causing further devastation and death.

The accuracy achieved by Bomber Command at Dresden was, to some extent, camouflaged by the horrifically indiscriminate results of the attack, and the dense concentration of bombs around the aim point was less immediately obvious than the devastation and huge death toll.

The sheer scale of this destruction and death at Dresden shook many

No 149 Sqn's NG361/OJ-E was one of the aircraft used in the infamous attack on Dresden. Typically anonymous, the aircraft lacks nose-art and, like most No 3 Group Lancasters, tail markings or outlined codes. A late-war build B I, NG361 survived the conflict and was struck off charge in 1947, having flown exclusively with No 149 Sqn *(via Bruce Robertson)*

No 550 Sqn's Plt Off D A Shaw (in the cockpit) is surrounded by members of his crew as they pose for a photo with their Lancaster (ED905/BQ-F), a long-serving aircraft illustrated in colour profile form both in this book and the previous Osprey Combat Aircraft Lancaster volume – it appears as No 103 Sqn's PM-X in the latter book. The bomber was finally written off in a landing accident whilst serving with No 1656 HCU at Lindholme on 20 August 1945, by which time it had flown 628+ hours
(via Bruce Robertson)

Allied observers, including Winston Churchill himself. On 28 March the Prime Minister penned a memo in which he observed that 'It seems to me that the moment has come when the question of bombing German cities simply for the sake of increasing terror (though under other pretexts) should be reviewed, otherwise we shall come into control of an utterly ruined land. I feel the need for more precise concentration on military objectives, rather than mere acts of terror and wanton destruction, however impressive'.

Churchill conveniently ignored the fact that the attack on Dresden had been a direct result of his own orders to attack eastern cities to support his ally, Stalin, and of the area bombing directives which he had hitherto supported with as much enthusiasm as had Harris. Moreover, by the time it was attacked, Dresden was less than 150 miles from the frontline, and was a vital hub for reinforcements and supplies using the roads and railways which it straddled, and because of its status as a vital port on the upper Elbe.

The AOC-in-C of Bomber Command was stung by Churchill's *volte face*, and felt understandably betrayed. Many believe that Dresden marked the point at which attitudes to Bomber Command began to shift, and that this change was largely due to the lead offered by Churchill.

Within months, Churchill was making his victory speech (in which Bomber Command did not merit a mention), while Harris's request for a campaign medal for his crews was flatly refused.

Although Churchill had distanced himself from the bombing offensive in the aftermath of the attack against Dresden, Harris continued to be guided by the spirit of the Directive No 22, which had been issued on Valentine's Day 1942. This had stated that 'the primary objective of your operations should now be focused on the morale of the enemy civil population, and in particular the industrial workers'. At the time, Charles Portal, the CAS, had issued his own clarification to the directive, explaining that 'The aiming points are to be the built up areas, not for example the dockyards or aircraft factories. This must be made quite clear if it is not already understood'.

Harris continued to attack his new targets in exactly this way, aiming for maximum destruction and maximum civilian casualties. Remaining targets had already been prioritised in such a way as to make this approach especially deadly. They were easy to find and identify, so that concentration of bombs around the aiming point became more and more intense. They also tended to have 'structural features' which made them 'especially suitable for fire attack', whether this meant a high degree of wooden construction or medieval narrow streets. Many towns were hit with appalling destruction, suffering relatively greater damage than even Dresden, although the 'headline' casualty figures were small because the towns themselves were often tiny.

Operation *Thunderclap* continued on 14/15 February, when 499 Lancasters and 218 Halifaxes attacked Chemnitz (later Karl Marx Stadt), with rather less destructive results. Wesel, a small town on the Rhine close to the Allied frontline, was then attacked daily between 16 and 19 February in an attempt to destroy its railway and road infrastructure.

Despite the success of Bomber Command's offensive against the enemy's oil facilities, the German defences could still inflict serious damage on the bombers. On 19/20 February Wg Cdr E A Benjamin, the Master Bomber on a raid to Böhlen, was downed by flak, and the Main Force bombing was, in consequence ineffective. While flak remained deadly throughout the war, the nightfighters flew less and less. When they did get airborne, however, they could be devastatingly effective.

On 20/21 February Bomber Command sent 514 Lancasters against Dortmund, losing 14 of them. Germany's leading nightfighter ace, Major Heinz-Wolfgang Schnaufer of NJG 4, downed two of the Lancasters that night, but worse was to follow the next night.

On 21/22 February 362 Lancasters were sent out against Duisberg, 36 against Worms and 166 Lancasters against the Mittelland Canal near Gravenhorst. This time Schnauffer shot down seven Lancasters in the space of only 17 minutes (his tally 121 night kills by war's end), while Hauptmann Johannes Hager of II./NJG 1 downed eight aircraft (he claimed 48 kills, all bar one at night), Hauptmann Heinz Rökker of 2./NJG 2 downed six (he claimed 64 kills, all bar one at night) and Oberfeldwebel Günther Bahr of I./NJG 6 shot down seven (he claimed 37 kills, all bar one at night).

During the rest of February Bomber Command Lancasters visited oil refineries at Gelsenkirchen and Osterfeld on the 22nd, Essen and Gelsenkirchen on the 23rd, Pforzheim on the night of the 23rd/24th, Kamen on the 24th, Dortmund on the 26th and Mainz on the 27th.

Operations continued in a similar vein in March, with attacks on Bocholt (22nd), Böhlen (5/6 and 20/21), Bottrop (15th and 24th), Bremen (21st), Chemnitz (5/6), Datteln (9th and 14th), Dessau (7/8), Dorsten (22nd), Dortmund (12th, 17th and 24th), Dülmen (22nd), Essen (11th), Farge (27th), Gelsenkirchen (5th, 13/14 and 19th), Hagen (15/16), Hamburg (8/9, 21/22 and 31st), Hamm (26th), Hanau (18/19), Hannover (25th), Harburg (7/8), Hemmingstedt (7/8 and 20/21), Hildesheim (22nd), Homberg (14/15), Kamen (3/4), Kassel (8/9), Köln (2nd), Lützkendorf (14/15), Mannheim (1st), Misburg (15/16), Münster (21st and 25th), Nuremberg (16/17), Osnabrück (25th), Paderborn (26th), Recklinghausen (20th), Rheine (21st), Salzbergen (6th), Sassnitz (6/7), Scholven (10th), Sterkrade (24th), Wanne-Eickel (4th), Wesel (6/7 and 23/24), Witten (18/19), Wuppertal (13th), Würzburg (16/17) and Zweibrucken (14/15).

Of these operations, two were particularly noteworthy. The attack on Essen on 11 March marked the largest number of aircraft despatched against a single target during the whole of the war. Essen had been attacked again and again, and was by then in ruins (although some early attacks had been costly failures) with some 7000 people having perished in the course of these air attacks, and with 300,000 more having fled the city for the countryside or neighbouring towns. In what was to be its last air raid, Essen lost another 897 people, and the city was occupied by the

Americans soon afterwards. All of Bomber Command's groups contributed aircraft to this daylight raid, and the total force of 1079 aircraft included 750 Lancasters, three of which were lost.

The record set at Essen was broken the following day (12 March) when 1108 aircraft, including 746 Lancasters, dropped a record tonnage of 4851 tons on Dortmund. Two Lancasters were lost.

The attack on the synthetic oil refinery at Lützkendorf on 14/15 March was smaller but more costly, and 18 of the 244 Lancasters sent out were lost (7.4 per cent). German nightfighter pilot Hauptmann Martin Becker, now leading IV./NJG 6, shot down eight Lancasters and a Halifax sent to attack Homberg.

The attack on Hamburg on 31 March also suffered heavy losses when Luftwaffe day fighters made what was, by then, a 'surprise intervention'. They hacked down eight of the 361 Lancasters and three of the 100 Halifaxes to give Bomber Command its last 'double figure' loss of the war, and probably marking the last occasion on which aircrew casualties exceeded casualties on the ground.

Many of the attacks mounted during March 'finished off' all industrial activity in the towns targeted. Sometimes these attacks marked the culmination of a series of raids, whereas on other occasions the target was receiving its first visit from Bomber Command. By March 1945, however, a single raid could be enough to knock out a target. Würzburg had been spared for most of the war, not least because it contained only a single 'Priority 2' target, in the shape of a power switching station, and lacked any 'Priority 1' targets at all. But under the new plans, it was a natural target, being easy to find and distinctive, with the town being situated close to an autobahn and a railway line. Finally, its narrow medieval streets made it almost a textbook target for incendiaries.

Thus, when No 5 Group despatched 226 Lancasters against the town on 16/17 March, Würzburg was hit by some 1000 tonnes of bombs (mainly incendiaries) in the space of 17 minutes. This caused 82 per cent destruction, and left 5000 dead.

Harry Evans flew on the mission against Würzburg, and recalled that it was 'a relatively easy target – wasn't like going to Essen or Berlin or any-where like that. We went there, we did what we had to do, apparently we took it out – another job "jobbed". So we didn't have to go back there another night. A lot of civilians may have been killed, but I can't say "that's tough" because they were there supporting the German war effort, whether they wanted to or not, and when you hear all the other things the Germans did . . . well I'm sorry, but at the time they were the enemy. It was total war and that's it as far as I'm concerned'.

But the bombers did not have it all their own way, and although the Luftwaffe was crippled by fuel shortages and the loss of many of its best aircrew, it could still sometimes get into the air and fight. On 3/4 March some 30 German intruders crossed the English coast and waited for the bombers returning from a raid on Ladbergen and mining operations off the Frisians. The Yorkshire-based Halifaxes suffered the heaviest losses that night, but German intruders also accounted for eight Lancasters, three of which had been returning from operations and five from training sorties. This marked the most spectacular success by German intruders of the whole war.

The Luftwaffe could also sometimes meet the bombers in open combat. On 25 March, for example, during a No 6 Group raid against Hannover, the bombers were attacked by some 30 Me 262s, whose pilots claimed to have shot down eight Lancasters – only one was actually lost, together with three Halifaxes which had been attacking Münster.

That same day No 630 Sqn launched a 14-aircraft daylight attack on Osnabrück. Unfortunately, as he taxied out, the unit's Master Bomber, Sqn Ldr G A Thorne, found that his aircraft had not been fuelled, and he was forced to wait while its tanks were topped up. He was able to catch up with the formation by routeing directly to the target, rather than using the dog-legged route which had been drawn up to avoid enemy defences. Thorne reached the target just in time to mark it, and won the DSO for his pains!

The low loss rate brought with it its own problems, as surplus aircrew on enlarged squadrons (growing from an establishment of 20 aircraft, plus four reserves, to 30 aircraft plus reserves) took longer to fly their allocated tour of operations. The plentiful supply of brand new aircraft even caused some headaches as crews lost their favourite (if weary and sub-modification standard) older aircraft. Sometimes squadrons made a case for retaining some older aircraft, especially where these had flown very large numbers of operations, or were approaching their 100th sortie.

Three new Lancaster units joined Bomber Command's order of battle during March, these comprising Nos 138 (the former Special Operations Executive support unit, which joined No 3 Group at Tuddenham, in Suffolk), 427 and 429 Sqns (which replaced their Halifaxes within No 6 Group at Leeming, in North Yorkshire). These were destined to be the last

Gp Capt Bonham-Carter, Waddington's station commander (second from left), with No 467 Sqn OC Wg Cdr W Brill DSO DFC (extreme right) show Air Vice Marshal H N Wrigley RAAF around the station's most distinguished Lancaster – B I R5868, which flew 137 missions with Nos 83 and 467 Sqns between June 1942 and war's end. The aircraft has been the centrepiece of the Bomber Command Hall at the RAF Museum at Hendon for over 20 years, having previously served as the gate guard at RAF Scampton
(via Bruce Robertson)

Lancaster units to see combat service, since Tholthorpe's two squadrons – Nos 420 and 425 Sqns – flew no operations after converting in April and May.

There were also heavy losses due to causes other than enemy action. Accidents were still common among the hastily (and some would say inadequately) trained wartime aircrew, while the sheer weight of numbers of aircraft at bomber airfields gave rise to problems. This was perhaps most dramatically illustrated on 17 April at East Kirkby, in Lincolnshire, where two 1000-lb bombs exploded as they were being loaded aboard a No 57 Sqn Lancaster. A 4000-lb bomb 'cooked off' in the ensuing conflagration, and flaming fragments caused neighbouring aircraft to explode – six were destroyed and fourteen more damaged. In human terms, 17 groundcrew were wounded, four of them fatally.

Just as it had attacked tactical and semi-tactical targets in support of the invasion of France, so too was Bomber Command pressed into service to support and prepare for the crossing of the Rhine. The Command mainly targeted important road and rail centres in the Rhineland and Ruhr, and one of the first such targets was Pforzheim, a vital road and rail link which lay between Karlsruhe and Stuttgart. Bomber Command launched 362 Lancasters against the town on 23/24 February.

During the attack the aircraft of Master Bomber Capt Edwin Swales SAAF of No 582 Sqn was badly hit, but he remained in the target area until satisfied that accuracy was good, and that the raid had achieved its objective. Swales stayed 'on station' directing the attack even after two nightfighter attacks had knocked out two engines and his rear guns. He then set course for France, remaining at the controls as his crew bailed out, before losing control of the crippled aircraft, in which he died. Swales won the VC for his cool heroism.

February saw the wholesale replacement of most of Bomber Command's group commanders, nominally to give command experience to a new generation of officers, but perhaps also to avoid the need for generous post-war recognition of men who were closely associated with what were already coming to be seen as the Command's worst excesses. Thus Air Vice Marshals Rice, Carr and Cochrane (of Nos 1, 4 and 5 Groups) were all replaced.

As well as attacking targets behind enemy lines, with the aim of disrupting Germany's ability to reinforce the front, Bomber Command also attacked frontline positions, sometimes within a few hundred yards of Allied troops. On the very eve of the Rhine Crossing, on 23 March as lead elements of the 1st Commando Brigade and the 51st Highland Brigade took up position around the town of Wesel, No 5 Group despatched 77 Lancasters (led by Pathfinder Mosquitos) against the town, in concert with a massive artillery barrage. That night, another attack was made by 195 Lancasters against the town. Wesel was razed, and the advancing commandos took it without difficulty.

April's targets included Bayreuth (11th), Bremen (22nd), Cham (17/18), Hamburg (8/9), Harburg (4/5), Heligoland (18th), Kiel (4/5 and 13/14), Komotau (18/19), Leipzig (10/11), Leuna (4/5), Lützkendorf (4/5 and 8/9 April), Molbis (7/8), Munich (19th), Nordhausen (3/4), Nuremberg (11th), Pilsen (16/17), Plauen (10/11), Potsdam (14/15), Regensburg (20th) and Schwandorf (16/17).

Wearing South African Air Force uniform, Capt Edwin Swales of No 582 Sqn is pictured before the 23 February 1945 mission which cost him his life, but which won him a posthumous VC *(via Bruce Robertson)*

The attack on Kiel on 9/10 April by 591 Lancasters was notably impressive, with a very high concentration of bombs around the two designated aim points. The raid mainly targeted German warships and U-boats, which were expected to make a run for Norway. The attack destroyed much port infrastructure and sunk 11 ships and two floating docks. The *Admiral Scheer* was hit and capsized, while the *Admiral Hipper* and the *Emden* were badly damaged. Three Lancasters were lost during the operation.

The attack on the Berlin suburb of Potsdam on 14/15 April by 500 Lancasters marked the first time four-engined bombers had entered the Berlin defence zone since the Battle of Berlin. Aimed at preventing reinforcement and easing the Red Army's passage to the centre of Berlin, it was also the last such attack. With much of Germany now in Allied hands, and with the Luftwaffe smashed, the raid was something of a milk-run, and only one Lancaster was lost.

No 5 Group ended its offensive against the German communications network with an attack on the railway yards at Komotau, in Czechoslovakia, on 18/19 April, all 114 of its Lancasters returning safely.

Five days before its surrender, and with the British XXX Corps preparing a final push, the port city of Bremen was attacked by 651 Lancasters, 100 Halifaxes and 16 Mosquitos on 22 April. The Master Bomber called off the attack after 195 aircraft had bombed because smoke and dust had by then entirely obscured the target.

The last day of the war for the Lancaster force was 25 April 1945, when it attacked coastal gun batteries on the island of Wangerooge (which covered the approaches to Bremen and Wilhelmshaven) and Hitler's mountain-top retreat at Berchtesgaden. The 158 Lancasters attacking

Seen amid the winter's snow at Strubby, in Lincolnshire, No 619 Sqn's 'D-Dog' (probably B III LM630/ PG-D) has an impressive but ill-defined bomb log and the name *DUMBO* on its nose. LM630 joined No 619 in July 1944, and flew on the final mission against Berchtesgarten at the end of the war *(via Phil Jarrett)*

Smoke billows from oil storage tanks at Bremen during a 21 March 1945 attack by 133 Nos 1 and 8 Group Lancasters, supported by a handful of Mosquitos. No aircraft were lost on this mission *(via Phil Jarrett)*

Lancaster B III LM739/HW-Z² completed 60 ops with No 100 Sqn between September 1944 and April 1945. It is seen here at Elsham Wolds following the unit's relocation from Grimsby (Waltham), the aircraft being joined by Sqn Ldr Hedley Scott DFC (in the cockpit), OC B Flt, and crew. The aircraft's last mission was to Hitler's 'Eagles Nest' at Berchtesgaden, this also being the final trip of the crew's operational tour and the last 'main force' Bomber Command operation of the war. LM739 was a No 1 Group leader for the raid, and to assist with daylight formation keeping, its vertical tail surfaces and wing tips were painted yellow, and its crew fired Verey cartridges and towed yellow pyrotechnic stars from the rear turret at specified points of the route. This Lancaster featured nose art on both sides, but a bomb log only on the port side of the fuselage. It was also fitted with a downward visibility blister beneath the bomb-aimer's position. Other details included extended exhaust flame shields, a large late-style bomb-aimer's bubble, a cockpit blister and nose window chute on the starboard side only and late style pitot mast and trailing aerial mounts. LM739 was struck off charge in October 1945 (*via Alastair McQuaid*)

Wangerooge (along with 308 Halifaxes and 16 Mossies) comprised ten from No 7 Sqn, eight from No 35 Sqn, ten from No 49 Sqn, sixteen from No 156 Sqn, four from No 405 Sqn, fifteen from No 419 Sqn, nine from No 424 Sqn, nine from No 427 Sqn, fifteen from No 428 Sqn, nine from No 429 Sqn, twelve from No 431 Sqn, nineteen from No 432 Sqn, ten from No 433 Sqn and fifteen from No 434 Sqn.

A slightly smaller force was despatched against Berchtesgaden. Although only 53 Lancasters of the 361 despatched pinpointed the primary target – Hitler's mountain retreat, known as the Berghof, it was totally destroyed, along with Göring's nearby residence, while the SS barracks were badly damaged.

Lancasters involved in this raid included seventeen aircraft from No IX Sqn, sixteen from No 12 Sqn, eight from No 44 Sqn, five from No 57 Sqn, sixteen from No 100 Sqn, twenty-four from No 101 Sqn, sixteen from No 103 Sqn, sixteen from No 150 Sqn, thirteen from No 153 Sqn, twenty-five from No 166 Sqn, sixteen from No 170 Sqn, ten from No 207 Sqn, six from No 227 Sqn, fourteen from No 300 Sqn and nine from No 405 Sqn.

That night (25/26 April 1945) 107 Lancasters (from Nos 50, 61, 83, 97, 106 and 189 Sqns) and 12 Mosquitos bombed an oil refinery at Vallo (Tonsberg), while four No 57 Sqn Lancasters mined Oslo Fjord. These were destined to be the Lancaster's last offensive missions.

Germany surrendered unconditionally on 7 May 1945 (with effect from 0001 hrs on 9 May). In the 11 months since D-Day, the British Army had lost 40,000 men, while Bomber Command had lost 10,000 airmen killed and 2128 aircraft. Germany had lost the war.

Bomber Command's performance in the last few months of the conflict was uncomfortably impressive, as cities and even small towns were reduced to rubble in a campaign which sometimes appeared disproportionate, if not actually pointless. Harris seemed to some to be

81

By the time *"WINNIE"* (B X KB760/NA-P) of No 428 Sqn returned to Canada, it was liberally bedecked with nose art. Flg Off R L Boyle was the aircraft's skipper for many of her 72 operations. Known as 'P for Panic' on the squadron, the aircraft ended up with crew nicknames (and sometimes portraits) adjacent to their positions. On the bomb door was inscribed 'P for Panic hit old Jerry, in every conceivable place, The war in Europe is over – gone, let's get cracking on that yellow race!' *(via Bruce Robertson)*

Flt Lt H G Topliss and some of his crew and groundcrew pose in front of their No 100 Sqn Lancaster ND644/HW-N at Waltham, on Humberside. The veteran aircraft flew some 112 missions (115 according to some sources) *(via Bruce Robertson)*

The Lancasters of the Polish-manned No 300 'Masovian' Sqn at Faldingworth, in Lincolnshire, were rarely photographed. This aircraft (BH-N) wears a small Polish air force insignia below the cockpit, and a No 1 Group gas detection patch further forward and lower down, but is otherwise anonymous. The unit began to run down in October 1946 and disbanded on 2 January 1947 *(via Aeroplane)*

gripped by a bloodthirsty and arguably excessive zeal, and critics began to wonder whether Britain had not 'lowered itself to Nazi standards' by waging such indiscriminate warfare against civilians. Similar ideas were expressed by Goebbels's propagandists.

Small wonder that the post-war RAF has chosen to focus on honouring the men who fought the Battle of Britain, and those involved in particular bombing actions (most notably the 'Dams Raid'), even though Bomber Command's sacrifice was greater, and its contribution arguably more important. It is easy to forget that the Command lost more men in one

The crew of No 75 (NZ) Sqn Lancaster PB820/JN-V at Mepal, in Cambridgeshire, during 1945. The unusual code presentation favoured by the New Zealand squadron is clearly evident *(via Phil Jarrett)*

With 84 'ops' under her belt, and 14 further flights carrying food to the Dutch or returning PoWs, *Edith* (LM577/HA-Q) is pictured at Chedburgh, in Suffolk, where she was the oldest, highest houred aircraft serving with resident No 218 Sqn, which disbanded in August 1945. This aircraft had initially served with No 622 Sqn *(via Bruce Robertson)*

night over Nuremberg than Fighter Command lost in the whole of the Battle of Britain.

It is also easy to forget that this was 'Total War', with little room or reason for quarter to be asked or extended, and it is perhaps worth reminding the reader that German civilians often lynched downed airmen if they got their hands on them. Moreover, Harris had fought and witnessed the carnage on the Western Front, and doubtless felt that the death of German civilians was preferable to the wholesale slaughter of another generation of British youth in the trenches, or in some hard fought advance on Berlin. Following the 1945 attack against Dresden, Harris had

summed up his attitude to the value of German civilian life by paraphrasing Bismarck;

'I do not believe that the whole of the remaining cities of Germany are worth the bones of one British Grenadier.'

The fact that Harris had fought in a war in which British military casualties exceeded one million dead probably also helped him to cope with what was, by comparison, the fairly modest Bomber Command casualty total of 55,000 dead. Bomber Command's losses were huge by World War 2 standards however, with a force which absorbed just seven per cent of Britain's military manpower suffering a quarter of Britain's war dead. Many of these casualties went to their deaths in the Lancaster.

The Lancaster ended the war flying more peaceful missions. Operation *Manna* saw units at Fiskerton, Stradishall and Witchford conducting intensive food-dropping missions to the starving Dutch populace, with 17 squadrons eventually flying 3156 sorties between 28 April and 10 May, and dropping 6684

tons of food. Large areas of Holland were still under German control then, but a local truce was arranged with the Wehrmacht commander in the area, and the Lancasters were able to operate unmolested. A veteran of the Dresden mission (HK696 of No 115 Sqn) had been despatched to Netheravon only ten days after the controversial operation to develop and practise food dropping techniques. The RAF eventually settled on a low

Groundcrewmen load canvas panniers of food sacks instead of bombs aboard a Lancaster as part of Operation *Manna*. Each Lancaster could carry five such panniers in its capacious bomb-bay, dropping them in a low-speed, low level pass. *Manna* saved hundreds of Dutch lives *(via Phil Jarrett)*

Food sacks stream from a No 115 Sqn Lancaster during Operation *Manna*. Lancasters from Nos 1, 3 and 8 Groups dropped 6684 tons of food in 2835 sorties, with the dropping zones marked by No 8 Group Mosquitos *(via Francis K Mason)*

Exhaust stains streak the top surfaces of this otherwise smart looking No XV Sqn Lancaster (NG358/LS-H), which wears distinctive yellow G-H Master Bomber markings on the inner and outer surfaces of its fins and rudders *(via Phil Jarrett)*

No 149 Sqn's PB509/OJ-C taxies out from its dispersal at Methwold, in Norfolk, during the spring of 1945. G-H Master Bomber PB509 is the subject of a colour profile in this volume *(via Phil Jarrett)*

altitude delivery (from 200 to 500 ft), dropping food from five panniers in the bomb-bay at a speed of between 110 and 120 knots, using half flap.

By the last day of full hostilities *Manna* was in full swing, with four No 7 Sqn Lancasters marking the Hague racecourse and three marking Valkenberg airfield for supply drops, while eight No 35 Sqn Lancasters marked an area of Rotterdam.

At the Hague the force committed included 17 No XV Sqn Lancasters as well as Nos 90 (17), 115 (26), 138 (16), 186 (15), 195 (16) and 218 (23) Sqns – a total of 130 aircraft.

Lancaster squadrons involved in the day's drops at Rotterdam comprised Nos 12 (19), 100 (15), 101 (26), 103 (19), 150 (18), 153 (17), 170 (20) and 300 (14) Sqns – a total of 148 aircraft.

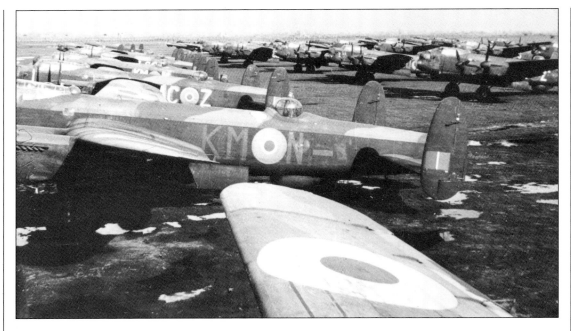

In addition to these, 26 No 75 Sqn Lancasters dropped supplies at Delft, 24 No 149 Sqn aircraft flew to Gouda and 31 No 166 Sqn 'heavies' delivered food, medicines and general supplies 'to the Dutch' at an unspecified location.

Operation *Exodus* began on 2 May, this seeing large numbers of Lancasters being used to ferry home PoWs from Europe. Stripped and fitted with rudimentary seating for 25 passengers, the Lancasters usually operated with a crew of six (the bomb aimer being omitted), and flew 29,000 round trips, bringing home 74,000 ex-PoWs in a 24-day period. The operation was marred by the loss of a single No 514 Sqn aircraft, which crashed on take off, killing everyone on board. Lancasters were later used for ferrying home soldiers and other personnel from Italy and the Mediterranean.

The Lancaster remained a mainstay of Bomber Command in the immediate aftermath of the war, although it would soon be replaced by

Lancasters are seen at Pomagliano, in Italy, during Operation *Exodus*. Some aircraft have had their dull red codes over-painted in white or light grey, while others retain their wartime colours. Many returning PoWs were able to view Europe at low level during their return flight, a hitherto undreamt of experience for most *(via Phil Jarrett)*

A line up of No 463 Sqn Lancasters load up with PoWs and soldiers at Bari, again in Italy, prior to the long, and long-awaited, flight back to 'Blighty'. The aircraft already wear the large underwing serials applied after the war *(via Phil Jarrett)*

Jubilant ex-PoWs celebrate their return to the UK after de-planing from _TAKE-IT-EASY!_. This group has clearly disembarked from a pair of Lancasters, which usually carried 25 passengers _(via Aeroplane)_

Before the atomic bomb brought the war in the Far East to a close, the RAF expected a major deployment of Lancasters as part of Tiger Force, to take part in the massive conventional bombing campaign which would accompany the invasion of Japan. Two aircraft were converted to evaluate an enormous dorsal 'saddle tank' to give the aircraft longer range, but this rendered the Lancaster's handling 'unacceptable' _(via Phil Jarrett)_

the Lincoln. The Command shrank dramatically, losing No 6 Group, whose squadrons returned to Canada, and ceding No 4 Group to Transport Command. Nos 5 and 8 Groups simply disbanded, surplus to the RAF's requirements.

Bomber Command ended the war with Harris at its head, although he would be quietly removed soon afterwards. The lack of recognition accorded to the Command, and its achievements, irked Harris, and he felt let down by the way in which Churchill (once a close ally) had distanced himself from the bombing offensive after Dresden.

It seems likely that Harris turned down a proferred peerage out of solidarity with his groundcrew (who were given no more than the Defence Medal, qualifying for no specific campaign medal), rather than never being offered the honour. He retired as scheduled in November 1945, several months short of qualifying for an air chief marshal's pension, although he was belatedly promoted to the honorary rank of Marshal of the Royal Air Force.

APPENDICES

APPENDIX A

AVRO LANCASTER SQUADRON IDENTITY CODES

AA No 75 (NZ) Sqn	F2 No 635 Sqn	MG No 7 Sqn	SW No 1678 HCF
AC No 138 Sqn	GG No 1667 HCU	MW No 101 Sqn (C Flt)	TC No 170 Sqn
AJ No 617 Sqn	GI No 622 Sqn	M9 No 1653 HCU	TK No 149 Sqn (C Flt)
AL No 429 Sqn	GP No 1661 HCU	NA No 428 Sqn	TL No 35 Sqn
AP No 186 Sqn (C Flt)	GT No 156 Sqn	ND No 1666 HCU	TV No 1660 HCU
AR No 460 Sqn	GZ No 12 Sqn (C Flt)	NF No 138 Sqn	UG No 1654 HCU
AS No 166 Sqn	HA No 218 Sqn	OF No 97 Sqn	UL No 576 Sqn
A2 No 514 Sqn (C Flt)	HW No 100 Sqn	OJ No 149 Sqn	UM No 626 Sqn
A3 No 1653 HCU	H4 No 1653 HCU	OL No 83 Sqn	UV No 460 Sqn
A4 No 115 Sqn (C Flt)	IL No 115 Sqn (C Flt)	OW No 426 Sqn	VN No 50 Sqn
A4 No 195 Sqn	IQ No 150 Sqn	PE No 1662 HCU	VR No 419 Sqn
A5 No 3 LFS	JE No 195 Sqn (C Flt)	PG No 619 Sqn	WL No 434 Sqn
BH No 300 Sqn	JF No 1654 HCU	PH No 12 Sqn	WP No 90 Sqn
BL No 1656 HCU	JI No 514 Sqn	PM No 103 Sqn	WS No IX Sqn
BM No 433 Sqn	JN No 75 (NZ) Sqn (C Flt)	PO No 467 Sqn	XH No 218 Sqn (C Flt)
BQ No 550 Sqn	JO No 463 Sqn	PT No 420 Sqn	XU No 7 Sqn (C Flt)
BS No 1651 HCU	J9 No 1668 HCU	P4 No 153 Sqn	XY No 90 Sqn (C Flt)
CA No 189 Sqn	KB No 1661 HCU	QB No 424 Sqn	XY No 186 Sqn
CE No 5 LFS	KC No 617 Sqn	QF No 1323 AGLT Flt	YJ No 617 Sqn
CF No 625 Sqn	KF No 1662 HCU	QO No 432 Sqn	YW No 1660 HCU
DH No 1664 HCU	KM No 44 Sqn	QQ No 1651 HCU	ZU No 1664 HCU
DJ No XV Sqn (C Flt)	KO No 115 Sqn	QR No 61 Sqn	ZL No 427 Sqn
DX No 57 Sqn	KW No 425 Sqn	QT No 57 Sqn (C Flt)	ZN No 106 Sqn
EA No 49 Sqn	K2 No 1668 HCU	QY No 1666 HCU	ZT No 97 Sqn (unused)
EK No 1656 HCU	LE No 630 Sqn	RC No 5 LFS	3C No 1 LFS
EM No 207 Sqn	LQ No 405 Sqn	RV No 1659 HCU	6O No 582 Sqn
EQ No 408 Sqn	LR No 1667 HCU	SE No 431 Sqn	9J No 227 Sqn
FD No 1659 HCU	LS No XV Sqn	SR No 101 Sqn	

Key

HCU - Heavy Conversion Unit
LFS - Lancaster Finishing School
AGLT – Automatic Gun-Laying Training Flight

APPENDIX B

THE LANCASTER IN BOMBER COMMAND'S FRONTLINE AIR ORDER OF BATTLE, APRIL 1945.

No 1 Group (HQ Bawtry)

Binbrook	No 460 Sqn	Lancaster
Elsham Wolds	No 100 Sqn	Lancaster
Elsham Wolds	No 103 Sqn	Lancaster
Elsham Wolds	No 576 Sqn	Lancaster
Faldingworth	No 300 Sqn	Lancaster
Hemswell	No 170 Sqn	Lancaster
Kelstern	No 625 Sqn	Lancaster
Kirmington	No 166 Sqn	Lancaster
Ludford Magna	No 101 Sqn	Lancaster
North Killingholme	No 550 Sqn	Lancaster
Scampton	No 153 Sqn	Lancaster
Wickenby	No 12 Sqn	Lancaster
Wickenby	No 626 Sqn	Lancaster

No 2 Group (HQ Huntingdon)
transferred to 2 Allied Tactical Air Force

No 3 Group (HQ Exning)

Chedburgh	No 218 Sqn	Lancaster
East Wretham	No 115 Sqn	Lancaster
Mepal	No 75 (NZ) Sqn	Lancaster
Methwold	No 149 Sqn	Lancaster
Mildenhall	No XV Sqn	Lancaster
Mildenhall	No 622 Sqn	Lancaster
Stradishall	No 186 Sqn	Lancaster
Tuddenham	No 90 Sqn	Lancaster
Tuddenham	No 138 Sqn	Lancaster
Waterbeach	No 514 Sqn	Lancaster
Witchford	No 115 Sqn	Lancaster
Wratting Common	No 195 Sqn	Lancaster

No 4 Group (HQ York)
Still fully Halifax equipped.

No 5 Group (HQ Grantham)

Balderton	No 227 Sqn	Lancaster
Bardney	No IX Sqn	Lancaster
Coningsby	No 83 Sqn	Lancaster
Coningsby	No 97 Sqn	Lancaster
East Kirkby	No 57 Sqn	Lancaster
East Kirkby	No 630 Sqn	Lancaster
Fulbeck	No 189 Sqn	Lancaster
Metheringham	No 106 Sqn	Lancaster
Scampton	No 57 Sqn	Lancaster
Skellingthorpe	No 50 Sqn	Lancaster
Skellingthorpe	No 61 Sqn	Lancaster
Spilsby	No 44 Sqn	Lancaster
Spilsby	No 207 Sqn	Lancaster
Syerston	No 49 Sqn	Lancaster

Waddington	No 463 Sqn	Lancaster
Waddington	No 467 Sqn	Lancaster
Woodhall Spa	No 617 Sqn	Lancaster

No 6 (RCAF) Group (HQ Allerton Park, Knaresborough)

Croft	No 431 Sqn	Lancaster
Croft	No 434 Sqn	Lancaster
East Moor	No 432 Sqn	Halifax
Leeming	No 427 Sqn	Lancaster
Leeming	No 429 Sqn	Lancaster
Linton-on-Ouse	No 408 Sqn	Lancaster
Linton-on-Ouse	No 426 Sqn	Halifax
Middleton St George	No 419 Sqn	Lancaster
Middleton St George	No 428 Sqn	Lancaster
Skipton-on-Swale	No 424 Sqn	Lancaster
Skipton-on-Swale	No 433 Sqn	Lancaster
Tholthorpe	No 420 Sqn	Lancaster (non op)
Tholthorpe	No 425 Sqn	Lancaster (non op)

No 8 (PFF) Group (HQ Wyton)
Partially equipped with the de Havilland Mosquito

Downham Market	No 635 Sqn	Lancaster
Gransden Lodge	No 405 Sqn	Lancaster
Graveley	No 35 Sqn	Lancaster
Little Staughton	No 582 Sqn	Lancaster
Oakington	No 7 Sqn	Lancaster
Upwood	No 156 Sqn	Lancaster

Note

By April 1945, Bomber Command's frontline strength was almost entirely dominated by the Lancaster, with three groups (Nos 1, 3 and 5) fully equipped and another (No 6) converting, and with the Lancaster serving alongside the Mosquito within No 8 PFF Group. The frontline thus included 13 Lancaster squadrons with No 1 Group, 12 with No 3 Group, 17 with No 5 Group, 11 with No 6 Group (two of which were still converting) and six with the Pathfinders, making a total of 59 squadrons. Bomber Command's only other 'heavies' were the Halifaxes of No 4 Group, totalling 11 squadrons, and two remaining Halifax units within No 6 Group.

COLOUR PLATES

Artwork notes

Wartime Lancasters had an unusually uniform appearance, with all but a handful wearing exactly the same dark green/dark earth/night camouflage, and with nose art and aircraft names being the exception rather than the rule, although aircraft with such decoration were more often photographed than their anonymous sisters, and have been more often portrayed by post-war artists. Some aircraft (especially those fitted with G-H or used as Master Bombers) did receive coloured tailfins late in the war, and yellow-edged code letters became common on No 5 Group aircraft. Configuration differed little, with a relative handful of aircraft having new Rose tail turrets or Martin mid-upper turrets, and with the Hercules radial engine being fitted to only about four per cent of the total Lancaster production run. A few aircraft were repainted in day bomber camouflage at the end of the war, but this was never common, and most Lancasters looked essentially the same as they had always done.

1
Lancaster B I LM220/WS-Y of No IX Sqn, Bardney, 1944

This Lancaster was fitted with bulged bomb-bay doors to allow it to carry a 12,000-lb *Tallboy* bomb for use against the *Tirpitz*. Its bomb log included 15 red bomb symbols for night operations and 27 yellow bombs denoting daylight operations, with bombs 39 and 40 bearing a superimposed R indicating a shuttle-bombing mission that landed in Russia. It also included two silhouettes of the *Tirpitz*, representing attacks on the German pocket battleship, during which LM220 was flown by Flt Lt W D Tweddle and crew. The nose art of an elderly gentleman with a pint of beer, and the slogan *GETTING YOUNGER EVERY DAY* referred to a contemporary advert for the products of William Younger's brewery. Although damaged in March 1945, LM220 survived the war, only to be scrapped at No 5 MU in November 1946. W4964/WS-J *Still Going Strong* was broadly similar in appearance, albeit with white tailfins, and this aircraft was commemorated by the RAF's Battle of Britain Memorial Flight, whose B I (PA474) wore this scheme between 1993 and 1999. No IX Sqn was worthy of such commemoration, having flown 3495 Lancaster sorties, and having lost 177 aircraft in the process. One squadron member, Flt Sgt G Thompson, was also awarded a posthumous VC.

2
Lancaster B I RA530/DX-Y of No 57 Sqn, East Kirkby, early 1945

Coloured tailfin stripes became common during the later part of the war, allowing aircraft to easily distinguish formation leaders, Master Bombers or aircraft equipped with G-H during daylight missions. In Nos 1 and 5 Groups, whole coloured

tailfins were sometimes used to indicate which base an aircraft was from. This H_2S-equipped Lancaster served with No 57 Sqn at East Kirkby until 20 March 1945, when it caught fire and hit a house at Stickney soon after taking off. Its red tail and black stripe denote a G-H aircraft. NX611, the Lancaster now owned by Lincolnshire farmers Fred and Harold Panton (who farm what used to be East Kirkby airfield) is today painted in No 57 Sqn colours (as DX-C *Just Jane*) on its starboard side.

3
Lancaster B I EE176/QR-M of No 61 Sqn, Skellingthorpe, 1945

MICKIE THE MOOCHER flew briefly with No 7 Sqn and then with No 97, before becoming one of three No 61 Sqn Lancasters which completed more than 100 missions, clocking up an incredible 122 combat operations (including aborts) before being retired to No 1653 HCU Unit (as H4-X) and then finally relegated to ground instructional duties with BOAC at Whitchurch. *MICKIE's* bomb log never showed more than 115 missions, although official records suggest that its tally may have been as high as 128 ops. This made the aircraft a natural choice for commemoration when the Battle of Britain Memorial Flight Lancaster was repainted at the end of the 20th Century. No 61 Sqn flew more Lancaster operations than any other frontline unit, and one of its pilots, Flt Lt Bill Reid, won a VC while serving with the unit in 1943.

4
Lancaster B I HK554/JN-F of No 75 Sqn, Mepal, August 1944

This No 75 (NZ) Sqn aircraft is typical of late-war Lancasters, being anonymous but for its serial and squadron codes. Aircraft with nose art were photographed more often, but were never common, except on some units. This aircraft does have an unusual code presentation, however, with JN placed aft of the roundel on both sides of the rear fuselage, forcing a cramped, two-row presentation of the serial number. This was standard on No 75 Sqn Lancasters, whether wearing AA or JN codes, the latter being used by C Flt only. HK554 flew as JN-Z and then as JN-F with No 75 (NZ) Sqn, before transferring to No 44 Sqn in the spring of 1945. It was struck off charge in March 1946. The bomber is seen here with the bulged bomb doors that were necessary in order for it to carry larger weapons like the 8000-lb HC bomb or the 12,000-lb *Tallboy*.

5
Lancaster B III NE181/JN-M of No 75 Sqn, Mepal, August 1944

While No 75 (NZ) Sqn used the codes AA, C Flt always used the letters JN. *THE CAPTAIN'S FANCY* survived 101 operations with the unit, some of the later trips skippered by Sqn Ldr Jim M Bailey, OC C Flt, who took over the aircraft from

Sqn Ldr Nick Williamson. The latter pilot had taken a fancy to the *'FANCY*, and flew six sorties in the aircraft, piloting NE181 on its 99th trip and his last mission of his tour. Bailey captained the aircraft on its 100th mission, to Krefeld, on 29 January 1945. The aircraft passed to No 514 Sqn, but did not fly operationally with its new owners. NE181 amassed a 101-mission bomb log, and was earmarked for delivery to New Zealand, but instead went to No 5 MU at Kemble. It was struck off charge in September 1947.

6
Lancaster B III PB532/HW-S^2 of No 100 Sqn, Elsham Wolds, April 1945
After service with No 550 Sqn, PB532 was passed to No 100 Sqn, where it was christened *SANTA AZUCAR*. The machine was the regular mount of Flt Lt O Lloyd-Davies, whose musical aptitude was reflected in the use of notes as mission symbols, and whose South American origins inspired the aircraft's name. No 100 Sqn moved from Waltham to Elsham Wolds on 1 April 1945, where PB532 served out the rest of the war. It was finally sold for scrap in July 1952 after service with the Telecommunications Flying Unit and the Transport Command Development Unit, followed by storage at No 15 MU.

7
Lancaster B I LL757/SR-W of No 101 Sqn, Ludford Magna, July 1944
OOR WULLIE was typical of No 101 Sqn's ABC-equipped Lancasters, with a profusion of antennas serving its high-powered transmitters, and quickly gaining a Rose tail turret housing a pair of 0.50-in machine guns. No 101 Sqn began using the Rose turret in May 1944, prior to it being officially cleared for service in September. This aircraft was the regular mount of Plt Off Waughman and his crew until it failed to return from an operation to Stettin on 30 August 1944 with 214 hours on the clock. Flt Lt W A M B Stewart and his nine-man crew were posted missing.

8
Lancaster B III ED888/PM-M^2 of No 103 Sqn, Elsham Wolds, November 1944
ED888 began its career with No 103 Sqn in May 1943, flying 54 sorties as PM-M and PM-M^2 before being taken over by No 576 Sqn when the latter unit formed from the C Flts of Nos 101 and 103 Sqns in December 1943. Re-coded as UL-V^2, and then as UL-M^2, 'Mike Squared' flew 77 further operations with No 576 Sqn, including the unit's first mission – to Berlin on 2/3 December 1943. Plt Off Jimmy Griffiths and his crew completed their 30th trip in ED888 before handing the veteran machine (in which they accounted for two enemy fighters) over to Plt Off J B 'Tinkle' Bell, whose first trip was also ED888's 100th mission. The aircraft later returned to No 103 Sqn for nine further sorties, taking the total to 140, the last being a mission to Köln on Christmas Eve 1944 in the

hands of Flg Off S L Saxe, or Flt Lt John Barnes, according to some sources. ED888 was damaged in an accident in February 1945 and was sent to No 10 MU. It had flown more operations than any other Lancaster, and had amassed more than 940 hours, but was scrapped in 1947. The DFC on the aircraft's huge bomb log was applied by the station commander at Elsham Wolds after the aircraft's 102nd trip.

9
Lancaster B III JB663/ZN-A of No 106 Sqn, Metheringham, 6 November 1944
KING OF THE AIR served with No 106 Sqn for its entire career, starting with a mission to Berlin on 26/27 November 1943. The bomber finally completed its 100th operation on 4 November 1944, and went on to fly 111 missions, retiring to No 24 MU in March 1945 before being struck off at No 15 MU Wroughton in October 1946. No 106 Sqn had fared less well, despite one of its members having won a VC. A mock funeral was held at Metheringham on 2 February 1946 as the unit disbanded.

10
Lancaster B III PB509/OJ-C of No 149 Sqn, Methwold, early 1945
No 149 'East India' Sqn traded its Short Stirlings for Lancasters in August 1944. With yellow bars on the tailfin indicating its status as a G-H Master Bomber (Nos 75, 90, 195, 218 and 622 Sqns used the same G-H markings), PB509 also featured very elaborate nose art consisting of a white horse drawing a Roman chariot, as well as a 30-mission bomb-log. The aircraft subsequently passed to No 186 Sqn as XY-Y, before going to No 1659 HCU. It was finally struck off charge in December 1945.

11
Lancaster B III ME812/AS-F of No 166 Sqn, Kirmington, June 1944
Plt Off Sid Coole and his crew flew *Fair Fighter's Revenge* into Linton-on-Ouse after an abortive mission against a V2 site. This aircraft (Coole's second *Fair Fighter's Revenge*) bore the image of a short-skirted and large-breasted miss bending a cane on its nose. Seen here with eight bomb symbols in its bomb log, ME812 went on to fly more than 100 operations (probably 105), most of them as P4-F of No 153 Sqn (from October 1944), and often in the hands of Sqn Ldr F R 'Paddy' Flynn. The aircraft retained its name and nose art and survived the war, being struck off charge at No 20 MU Aston Down on 25 October 1946.

12
Lancaster B III PB480/TC-G^2 of No 170 Sqn, Hemswell, March 1945
This aircraft, flown by Flt Lt Bob Chandler and crew, carried a distinctive circular No 1 Group gas detection patch on its nose, and artwork of all seven of Disney's dwarves, together with the legend *Hi Ho! Hi Ho! It's off to work we go*. This

was painted on canvas by wireless operator Sgt Ron Woodin, and was then stuck onto the aircraft's aluminium skin. PB480 had served with No 625 Sqn as CF-J before going to No 170 (which formed from a flight of No 625), and ended its days as a ground instructional airframe (6710M).

13
Lancaster B III ND758/A4-A of No 195 Sqn, Witchford, October 1944
No 115 Sqn's C Flt applied its assigned A4 code with the '4' in a much smaller size, as seen here. When No 195 Sqn formed from this flight in October 1944, it retained both the code and the method of presentation. *The Bad Penny!* (an ex-No 75 (NZ) Sqn machine) was flown by Flg Off D S McKechnie and his crew, before being passed to No 3 LFS in November 1944. The aircraft then flew with No 1653 CU and was struck off in May 1947.

14
Lancaster B II LL725/EQ-Z of No 408 Sqn, Linton-on-Ouse, 24 April 1944
ZOMBIE of No 408 Sqn bore a bomb log which included two Swastikas representing enemy fighters shot down by the aircraft's gunners, five bomb symbols indicating targets in Germany and a row of Maple leaves representing targets in the occupied countries of Europe. The nose art portrayed a cloaked and cookie-toting skeleton, applied by rear gunner Sgt George Allen. *ZOMBIE* joined No 408 Sqn after brief service with No 423 Sqn, and was usually skippered by Flg Off E M C Franklin. It eventually went missing during a mission against Hamburg on 15/16 March 1944. No 408 Sqn's B IIs were duly replaced by Merlin-engined B Xs, one of which (FM212/EQ-W) survived the war and is today displayed on a pole in Windsor, Ontario.

15
Lancaster B X KB732/VR-X of No 419 Sqn, Middleton St George, 1945
The Lancaster B X was essentially a B III built under licence by Victory Aircraft Ltd at Malton, Ontario. *X-TERMINATOR* was one of the first 75 aircraft built in Canada, so it used US Packard Merlin 38 engines, whereas later aircraft used the Merlin 224. This machine flew 75 operations with No 419 Sqn before returning to Canada on 5 June 1945. No 419 disbanded in Yarmouth, Nova Scotia, in September 1945. The aircraft was struck off in April 1948, surplus to requirements. Sister aircraft KB726/VR-A was the bomber in which Plt Off Andrew Mynarski won his VC, and the Canadian Warplane Heritage Museum flies its airworthy B X (FM213) in these colours.

16
Lancaster B I NG347/QB-P of No 424 Sqn, Skipton on Swale, 1945
NG347's nose art showed a young lady about to remove her bikini top, beside which were painted representations of the DFC and DFM medal

ribbons – awards made to members of the aircraft's crew. The *PICCADILLY PRINCESS* served only with No 424 Sqn, and was eventually struck off charge in May 1947. No 424 traded its Halifaxes for Lancasters in January 1945, and flew 29 raids with the new type, totalling 388 sorties. It lost five Lancasters through enemy action, and two more in operational accidents. Post-war the unit moved to No 1 Group in August 1945 but disbanded on 15 October 1945.

17
Lancaster B X KB848/NA-G of No 428 Sqn, Middleton St George, May 1945
FIGHTIN' PAPPY had a devil's head insignia on its nose, which was surrounded by 30 'sunburst' mission symbols by the time it flew back to Canada on 31 May 1945. The aircraft was ferried home by Flt Lt G Cox and his crew, the aircraft leaving Middleton St George on 31 May and staging to Yarmouth, Nova Scotia, via the Azores, arriving on 8 June. KB848 was later modified as a Mk 10 DC drone carrier, carrying Ryan Firebee target drones until retirement in April 1964. The aircraft's nose was then preserved by the Canadian National Aeronautical Collection at Rockcliffe, Ottawa. Like many Canadian-built B Xs, *FIGHTIN' PAPPY* had a Martin mid-upper turret with a pair of 0.50-in machine guns mounted further forward than the usual turret.

18
Lancaster B X KB864/NA-S of No 428 Sqn, Middleton St George, May 1945
On the port side, *Sugar's BLUES* carried a glamorous girl on its nose, adapted from a Vargas painting in the August 1944 issue of *Esquire*, and its bomb log was presented in the form of diving maidens. This was applied by Sgt Tom Walton, a No 428 Sqn wireless operator and air gunner. To starboard, the same aircraft wore a different badge, with a scythe-wielding cartoon ghost dropping a large red bomb. KB864 returned to Canada on 2 June 1945, flown by its regular skipper, Flt Lt Bob Laturner, and was struck off charge on 16 January 1947. Some of the unit's aircraft did survive, and KB944, a sister aircraft which flew operationally with No 425 Sqn, is today painted in No 428 Sqn markings as NA-P and displayed at the Canadian National Aviation Museum at Ottawa. KB864's markings, meanwhile, are carried by the Lancaster cockpit section held by the Nanton Air Museum.

19
Lancaster B I ME649/AR-J[2] of No 460 Sqn Binbrook, 1944
No 460 Sqn replaced its Halifaxes with Lancasters in October 1942. A No 1 Group squadron, No 460 moved from Breighton to Binbrook in May 1943, and then to East Kirkby immediately after the war. When pictured, this Lancaster had flown 63 missions. It went missing during a raid on Essen on 12/13 December 1944. ME649's replacement as 'J-Jig[2]' was rare interim B VII NX560.

20
Lancaster B I ME701/JO-F of No 463 Sqn, Waddington, 1944
No 463 Sqn was the third RAAF Lancaster unit in Bomber Command, and it soon gained a reputation for efficiency and good morale. Formed at Waddington on 25 November 1943 from No 467 Sqn's C Flt, the unit remained there until July 1945, when it moved to Skellingthorpe. ME701 *Whoa Bessie* was damaged beyond repair by flak over Beauvoir on 29 June 1944, the aircraft being written off after landing safely at base.

21
Lancaster B III ED611/JO-U of No 463 Sqn, Waddington, June 1944
UNCLE JOE of No 463 Sqn is portrayed as it appeared at the start of its 100th operation, with *100 UP TONIGHT* chalked on the nose below the Joseph Stalin nose art. Stalin was superimposed on a red star, and red and yellow stars formed the aircraft's bomb log. The *UNCLE JOE* nose art had been applied while the aircraft was serving with No 44 Sqn (as KM-J), but the use of stars as a background and as a 'bomb log' began with the RAAF unit. Eventually transferred to No 101 Sqn, ED611 had the Stalin artwork painted on to a red shield, and 113 mission marks were applied as rows of crossed Union Jacks and Red Flags. A lucky aircraft, *UNCLE JOE* was eventually retired from operations and passed to the Bombing Trials Unit, before being struck off charge in January 1947.

22
Lancaster B I RF141/JO-U of No 463 Sqn, Waddington, May 1945
Hoping to repeat *UNCLE JOE's* success, No 463 Sqn named its next 'U-Uncle' after the earlier aircraft. *"UNCLE JOE" AGAIN* joined No 463 Sqn in February 1945, and carried a similar portrait of Stalin, albeit superimposed on a red flag instead of a red star. Stars were applied below the cockpit as a mission tally. This aircraft also survived the war, being retired to No 22 MU at Silloth in October 1945 and scrapped in March 1948.

23
Lancaster B I LM130/JO-N of No 463 Sqn, Waddington, early 1945
Flg Off Ray Hattam's *NICK THE NAZI NEUTRALIZER* was one of the No 463 Sqn aircraft adapted to carry cameramen from the RAF's Film Unit, and thus accompanied special attacks (like those against the *Tirpitz*) as well as participating in normal, routine, 'Main Force' operations. *NICK'S* bomb log used mission symbols which consisted of suitably satanic tridents in red and yellow. The aircraft crashed at Metheringham on 11 March 1945.

24
Lancaster B I DV372/PO-F of No 467 Sqn, Waddington, October 1944
OLD FRED completed 49 operations with No 467

Sqn, latterly in the hands of Flt Lt Jim Marshall, before going to No 1651 HCU at Woolfox Lodge, with whom it suffered a major accident on 4 October 1945. The aircraft's nose art (which was over-painted during the aircraft's time with the heavy conversion unit) consisted of a cartoon wolf, with the legend *OLD FRED* on a scroll which linked the RAF and Australian flags. The bomb log was applied in the form of miniature roundels. The full code of PO-F was repeated on the nose, under the front turret. DV372's nose ended up in London's Imperial War Museum, where the artwork was re-discovered and uncovered, and where the nose section remains on display to this day. One of the aircraft's sister-ships on No 467 Sqn also survives in a London museum, PO-S gracing the Bomber Command Hall within the RAF Museum at Hendon.

25
Lancaster B II DS842/JI-F of No 514 Sqn, Waterbeach, Spring 1944
No 514 Sqn was the only unit to form from scratch with the Lancaster II, the remaining operators converting from other aircraft types. No 514 also had the distinction of being the last unit to fly an operation with the type. *FANNY FERKIN II*, the mount of Plt Off Bob Langley and his crew, attracted the attention of the propaganda photographers when it diverted to Deenethorpe, home of the Eighth Air Force's 401st Bomb Group. The aircraft, fitted with bulged bomb-bay doors and an FN 64 ventral turret, served until May 1944, and then went to No 1668 HCU, before being struck off charge in March 1945.

26
Lancaster B III ED905/BQ-F of No 550 Sqn, North Killingholme, November 1944
ED905 was illustrated twice in the first Osprey Combat Aircraft volume on the Lancaster, which gives some impression of this aircraft's astonishing longevity. After service with No 103 Sqn (as PM-X) and No 166 Sqn (as AS-X), the bomber joined No 550 Sqn in the summer of 1944. With a new nose-art obscuring the crossed British and Belgian flags previously carried, the aircraft was named *PRESS ON REGARDLESS*. The new artwork included a heraldic shield dominated by a pretty girl and a pint of beer, and the motto *AD EXTREMUM*. Flt Lt D A Shaw took the aircraft on its 100th operation (to Bochum) on 4/5 November 1944. ED905 was eventually transferred to No 1 LFS and then to No 1656 HCU, with whom it suffered an undercarriage collapse at Lindholme and was struck off charge on 20 August 1945.

27
Lancaster B III PA995/BQ-V of No 550 Sqn, North Killingholme, 1944
Formed in November 1943 from No 100 Sqn's C Flt, No 550 Sqn moved from Waltham to North Killingholme on 3 January 1944. By the time Flg Off George Blackler completed his 37th, and final,

operation (his 27th in this aircraft) on 5/6 March 1945, *The Vulture Strikes* must have seemed like a 'lucky kite', since it was also the aircraft's 100th trip. But even in March 1945, with the loss rate plummeting, and even in an aircraft that had completed 100 operations, Bomber Command was still a dangerous place to serve. Flg Off C J Jones and two of his crew found this out on 7 March, when they took PA995 on its 101st and final trip, going down during a mission to Dessau.

28
Lancaster B I LM227/UL-I of No 576 Sqn, Elsham Wolds, 1945

This unnamed Lancaster was one of at least three No 576 Sqn aircraft which completed 100 operations or more. Its simple nose art consisted of Saturn and a trail of stars above a huge bomb log. The aircraft was captained by Flt Lt Stuart Simpson during the final weeks of the war, and its record included 39 day bombing missions and seven Operation *Manna* food-dropping sorties. LM227 was finally struck off charge on 19 October 1945.

29
Lancaster B I DV385/KC-A of No 617 Sqn, Woodhall Spa, mid 1944

DV385 was one of the aircraft delivered to No 617 Sqn to replace the 'Provisioning' Lancasters which had survived the 'Dams Raid', although in the event, several of these were destined to remain in use with the unit, or with Scampton's Station Flight, until the end of the war, mainly dropping *Tallboys* and 12,000-lb HC bombs and carrying supplies for the SOE. Five such veterans of Operation *Chastise* remained in use at the beginning of 1945, comprising the aircraft flown by Maltby, Martin, Knight, Shannon and Gibson (ED906, ED909, ED912, ED929 and ED932). *Thumper Mk III*, by contrast, was a standard Lancaster B I, albeit with bulged doors to allow the carriage of a *Tallboy* or a 12,000-lb HC bomb. The aircraft's bomb-log included mission marks with a 'D' indicating D-Day missions, and a swastika denoting an enemy fighter shot down. Mainly flown by Flt Lt R H Knights and his crew, *Thumper Mk III* participated in two attacks on the *Tirpitz* and was finally struck off charge in April 1945 at No 46 MU.

30
Lancaster B I ED763/KC-Z of No 617 Sqn, Woodhall Spa, October 1944

'HONOR' participated in three attacks on the *Tirpitz*, being flown by Flt Lt Stuart Anning for the third of these, on 12 November 1944. The aircraft was fitted with the SABS (Stabilised Automatic Bomb Sight) used only by No 617 Sqn, and lacked the normal mid-upper turret. ED763 was used for a number of attacks against viaducts and other targets, dropping both the 12,000-lb HC bomb and the *Tallboy*. The aircraft was struck off charge on 14 May 1945.

31
Lancaster B I (Special) PD119/YZ-J of No 617 Sqn, Woodhall Spa, Spring 1945

PD119 was one of a batch of 32 B I (Special) aircraft specifically built to carry the 22,000-lb *Grand Slam* bomb, 24 bombers eventually being issued to No 617 Sqn. Delivered during January-March 1945, the aircraft were painted in day bomber camouflage, and lacked all but the rear turret. This carried a reduced ammunition load, to save weight. Squadron codes were repeated on the top surfaces of the tailplanes, as pioneered by No 83 Sqn and other units. This particular aircraft flew at least three operational *Grand Slam* missions in the hands of No 617 Sqn's CO, Gp Capt J E Fauquier RCAF, attacking the Arnsburg Viaduct on 19 March, the Bremen bridge on 23 March and U-Boat pens at Farge on 27 March. After service with Nos 156 and 15 Sqns, the aircraft went to the Royal Aircraft Establishment at Farnborough, where it was eventually struck off charge in September 1950.

32
Lancaster B III EE134/PG-Y of No 619 Sqn, Strubby, October 1944

The unnamed EE134 bore an unusual mock-heraldic crest on its nose, containing a skull and other portents of doom, below which was an impressive bomb log recording the bare bones of an operational career with Nos 49 and 619 Sqns, including no less than ten trips to Berlin. After service with No 619 Sqn, the aircraft passed to No 5 LFS, where it flew as CE-O until struck off charge at the end of March 1945. The aircraft ended its days as a tethered ground rig with inboard engines only, used for fire detection and extinguisher trials by Rolls-Royce at Hucknall.

33
Lancaster B I LL966/LE-P of No 630 Sqn, East Kirkby, late 1944

LL966 served as a G-H Master Bomber with No 630 Sqn, and so featured a black horizontal bar across its fin and rudder. Unusually for a No 630 Sqn aircraft, it did not have its individual letter code repeated in a square on the nose. LL966 was one of three bombers lost on 14/15 February 1945 during an attack on Rositz. NX611, the Lancaster now owned by Lincolnshire farmers Fred and Harold Panton (who farm what used to be East Kirkby airfield), is today painted in No 630 Sqn colours (as LE-C) on its starboard side.

Back Cover
Lancaster B VI ND673/F2-V of No 635 Sqn, Downham Market, 1944

Formed at Gravely on 20 March 1944 as a Pathfinder Lancaster squadron, No 635 received five Lancaster B VIs from July 1944, briefly using these to augment its B Is and B IIIs, losing one before passing the remainder on to trials units in October and November. With their 1635 hp Merlin 85 engines, the B VIs were used as Master

Bombers, and for very high altitude jamming and spoofing missions, carrying extra 'Window', improved H$_2$S and 12 unidentified jammers (probably *Carpet II* or *Carpet Sweeper*, designed to disrupt Wurzburg GCI radar). The aircraft (JB675/F2-U, JB713/F2-Z, ND418/F2-Q, ND558 and ND673/F2-V) were fitted with an array of dipole antennas under the cockpit, and had no dorsal turrets. ND673 flew 25 operations with No 635 Sqn – more than any of the other frontline B VIs – and subsequently passed to the RAE. The aircraft featured yellow identification stripes on its tailfins. One other B VI (JB675) was also used by No 7 Sqn as MG-O, and a third (JB713) by No 405 Sqn as LQ-P.

BIBLIOGRAPHY

HOLMES, HARRY, *Avro Lancaster, The Definitive Record*. Airlife, 1997
MASON, FRANCIS K, *The Avro Lancaster*. Aston, 1989
FRANKS, RICHARD A, *The Avro Lancaster, Manchester and Lincoln (Modellers Datafile No 4)*. SAM Publications, 2000
FLYPAST SPECIAL, *Lancaster, A Tribute to Britain's Most Famous Bomber*. Key, 1998
MACKAY, R S G, *Lancaster, in Action*. Squadron/Signal, 1982
BUSHELL, SUE J, *Avro Lancaster, Mighty Hero of the Night Sky*. Maze Media, 1996
GARBETT, MIKE AND GOULDING, BRIAN, *The Lancaster At War*. Ian Allan, 1971
GARBETT, MIKE AND GOULDING, BRIAN, *The Lancaster At War 2*. Ian Allan, 1979
GARBETT, MIKE AND GOULDING, BRIAN, *The Lancaster At War 3*. Ian Allan, 1984
GARBETT, MIKE AND GOULDING, BRIAN, *The Lancaster At War 4 - Pathfinder Squadrons*. Ian Allan, 1990
GARBETT, MIKE AND GOULDING, BRIAN, *The Lancaster At War 5 Fifty Years On*. Ian Allan, 1995
GARBETT, MIKE AND GOULDING, BRIAN, *Avro Lancaster I, Profile No 65*. Profile Publications, undated
ROBERTSON, BRUCE, *Avro Lancaster II, Profile No 235*. Profile Publications, undated
GARBETT, MIKE AND GOULDING, BRIAN, *Avro Lancaster in Unit Service*. Osprey Aircam No 12, 1968
MASON, FRANCIS K, *Major Archive Avro Lancaster B Mks I-III*. Cerberus/Container, undated
PATTERSON, DAN AND DICK, RON, *Lancaster RAF Heavy Bomber*. Airlife, 1996
GOULDING, BRIAN, GARBETT, MIKE AND PARTRIDGE, JOHN, *Story of a Lanc*. Lincolnshire Aviation Heritage Centre, 1991
JACKSON, A J, *Avro Aircraft Since 1908*. Putnam, 1990
THETFORD, OWEN, *Aircraft of the Royal Air Force since 1918*. Putnam, 1995
BOWYER, MICHAEL J F, *Aircraft for the Many*. PSL, 1995
BOWYER, MICHAEL J F, *Bombing Colours, RAF Bombers, their markings and operations, 1937-73*. PSL, 1973
FOCHUK, STEPHEN M, *Metal Canvas, Canadians and World War II Aircraft Nose Art*. Vanwell/Canadian War Museum, 1999
HMSO, *Bomber Command*. undated
HMSO, *Bomber Command Continues*. 1943
HASTINGS, MAX, *Bomber Command*. Michael Joseph, 1979
OVERY, RICHARD, *Bomber Command 1939-45*. HarperCollins, 1997
TERRAINE, JOHN, *The Right of the Line*. Hodder, 1985
HARVEY, MAURICE, *The Allied Bomber War, 1939-1945*. Spellmount, 1992
FREEMAN, ROGER A, *Raiding the Reich*. Arms & Armour Press, 1997
DELVE, KEN, AND JACOBS, PETER, *The Six Year Offensive*. Arms & Armour Press, 1992
BOWYER, CHAZ, *Bomber Barons*. Kimber, 1983
BOWYER, CHAZ, *For Valour*. Grub St, 1992
TURNER, JOHN FRAYN, *VCs of the Air*. Airlife, 1993
MOYES, PHILIP, *Bomber Squadrons of the RAF and their Aircraft*. MacDonald, 1964 and 1976
HALLEY, JAMES J, *The Squadrons of the Royal Air Force*. Air-Britain Publications.
JEFFORD, C G, Wg Cdr, *RAF Squadrons*. Airlife, 1988
DELVE, KEN, *The Source Book of the RAF*. Airlife, 1994
STURTIVANT et al, *Royal Air Force Flying Training and Support Units*. Air-Britain, 1998
BIDDLE, TAMI DAVIS, 'British and American Approaches to Strategic Bombing', published in *Air Power in Theory and Practise by John Gooch*. Cass, 1995
PARKS, W HAYS, 'Precision and Area Bombing - who did which, and when?', published in *Air Power in Theory and Practise by John Gooch*. Cass, 1995
BENNETT, D C T, AVM, *Pathfinder*. Frederick Muller, 1958
GIBSON, E M, *Enemy Coast Ahead* . Michael Joseph, 1946

INDEX

References to illustrations are shown in **bold**. Plates are shown with page and caption locators in brackets.